"The Search for Identity"

by

Arnold Theodore Olson

Lincoln Christian
University Library

THE EVANGELICAL FREE CHURCH OF AMERICA

FREE CHURCH PRESS
1515 East 66th Street
Minneapolis, MN 55423

© Copyright 1980
by
FREE CHURCH PRESS
All rights reserved

Every effort has been made to identify and acknowledge the source of material used. If additional information is obtained, it will be included in subsequent editions.

ISBN 0-911802-46-0
LIBRARY OF CONGRESS CATALOG NUMBER: 80-66030

Printed in the United States of America
by Free Church Press, Minneapolis, MN 55423

Lincoln Christian
University Library

To Carrie Lynn

Preface

History is more than a listing of dates and a review of events. Although the importance of these must not be minimized, history also involves ideals, emotions, and values that cannot be quantized. It has the narrative of a good story and contains a wealth of colorful personalities, exciting dialogue, and dramatic incidents. I have tried to capture some of these in this volume.

The early believers coming out of the great spiritual revivals in Scandinavia and from among the Scandinavian immigrants in America not only searched and found in the Scriptures the divine plan for salvation but discovered a plan for the fellowship of believers and a pattern for a local congregation. In the beginning there were no great movements away from the State Church which in those countries was of the Lutheran faith. But as the new converts matured in their knowledge of the Bible, they found that the Church had moved far away from the Word of God and even some of the teachings of Martin Luther who preached that man was justified by faith and all believers were priests. They rebelled against a government-appointed clergy, which exercised authority over the religious lives of the citizens, and sought to return to the New Testament truth that the ministry belongs to all believers alike, without any discrimination. They also found in their study of the Scriptures that the whole church was involved in the policy-making process as well as in the appointment of leaders, the acceptance or rejection of applicants for membership in a fellowship, the expulsion of members, the discipline of fellow members, and the setting apart of believers for special assignments in the work of their Lord and Savior.

Did not the Bible say that the believers were a royal

priesthood; that there was neither Jew nor Greek, bond nor free, male nor female, circumcision nor uncircumcision, Barbarian, Scythian? Were not all one in Christ? While God did give different gifts to believers, were they not for the purpose of serving and not to be used in lording it over the body of Christ? Were they not all given by the same Spirit?

When it became necessary to fill the vacancy in the twelve caused by the departure of Judas, did not the eleven leave it to the 120 brethren, with no evidence that the women were excluded, to make the final choice after proposing two names, Joseph and Matthew? (Acts 1:23-26) Did not the entire group choose Matthew (Acts 1:26)? Chrysostom (347-407) also known as John of Antioch, in his commentary on Acts 1 notes: "Peter did everything here with common consent; nothing by his own will or authority. He left the judgment to the multitude, to secure their respect to the elected, and to free himself from every invidious reflection. He did not himself appoint the two, it was the act of all."

According to Acts 6 it was the "whole group of believers" who appointed the deacons. In Acts 13, while the first missionaries were sent forth by a few in obedience to God's command, Paul and Barnabas recognized that they were servants of the church. Upon their return to Antioch they "rehearsed to the people of the church all that God had done with them and how he had opened a door of faith to the Gentiles" (Acts 14:27). When the believers at Antioch faced a question of policy regarding whether or not they had to enter the fellowship through the rituals and customs of Judaism it was the church that brought the leaders "on their way" to seek counsel from the older fellowship in Jerusalem (Acts 15). Upon their arrival they were "received of the church, and of the apostles, and of the elders" (v. 4). The matter was first discussed in committee but then presented to "the multitude" (v. 12). The final resolution "pleased the apostles, elders, with the whole church" (v. 22). This was done only after the whole matter was also considered in the light of "where stands it written." "To this agree the words of the prophets as it is written" (v. 15). The letter of recommendation (not command) sent to Antioch was from "the brethren" as well as the leaders and eventually presented to the "multitude who rejoiced for the message of encouragement" (v. 22-31).

Regarding the acceptance or rejection of those who sought to become part of a fellowship, it was the "whole church," not a bishop, elders or a board of deacons, who made the decisions. The company of believers was given the authority to (a) excommunicate; (b) deny the right hand of fellowship. Charges against members, if not resolved by the parties concerned or with the help of witnesses, should be brought before the "whole church"; and if the guilty party "neglected the church, let him be as a heathen man or a publican" (Matt. 18:15-17). The same authority is given in I Corinthians 5 where, in the case of immorality, it was those "gathered together" who were to deliver such a one "to Satan for the destruction of the flesh that the spirit may be saved in the day of the Lord" (v. 4, 5).

Jesus taught that greatness was not determined by positions of authority but by service: "Whosoever will be great among you, let him be your minister, and whosoever will be chief among you let him be your servant" (Matt. 20:26, 27). He also taught: "For one is your master, even Christ, and all ye are brethren. And call no man your Father upon the earth; for one is your Father, which is in heaven. Neither be ye called masters; for one is your Master, even Christ. But he that is greatest among you shall be your servant. And whosoever shall exalt himself shall be abased; and he that shall humble himself shall be exalted" (Matt. 23:8-13). The founders had difficulty accepting the rite of ordination, lest one believer be exalted above another. Did not Paul look upon himself as "less than least of the saints" (Eph. 3:8)? It was not the load of a high office that weighed him down, but the "care of the churches" (II Cor. 11:28). This he states after summarizing the many sufferings he had experienced as evidence of his being a minister. Further, he left the handling of donated funds for the poor in Jerusalem to one, not appointed by himself but chosen by the churches (II Cor. 8:19).

As to ordination, though the act of laying on of hands in setting one apart for some special ministry was done by church leaders, (I Tim. 4:14) the proof of the rightness of that action was to be "seen by all" (v. 15).

Recognizing the authority of the membership in the local congregation, the founders also discovered that local groups were tied to one another through correspondence, such as the epistles; itinerant preachers; special projects; such as assisting the victims of poverty in Jerusalem (II Cor. 9, Romans 15:26); and common policies (Acts 15). The question for them became, how can we best, in our day, work out a plan for following the New Testament pattern as we see it? How can we work together as separate groups of believers without surrendering the authority in the local congregation?

It is this search of the Scriptures, study of church history, and appraisal of the contemporary church scene at the end of the last century by the pioneers to find the most practical way to develop a Biblical plan for interchurch relationships that this book is all about.

It is my fervent prayer that as we become increasingly aware of our roots we may become better and more worthy branches.

Arnold Theodore Olson

Minneapolis, MN
October 1, 1979

Contents

Chapter I

THE STEPCHILDREN OF THE REFORMATION

With very few exceptions, those denominations in America dominated by the white race have their roots in the countries of Europe. These include the historic mainline church bodies such as the Reformed, Lutheran, Episcopalian and Presbyterian. Others such as the Moravian, Mennonite, Methodist, and Congregational were the result of dissenter movements coming out of the State Churches of Europe. Among these would be the Evangelical Free Church.

The Reformers stopped somewhere between the Roman Catholic Church and the New Testament. Roman Catholicism, for example, could not tolerate a church within the church. From the time Constantine (313) made Christianity the official religion of the State, the persecutions of the Christians by the pagans was turned around and the church became the persecutor, first of the pagans, and later of the Christian dissenters. The church used governmental authority to coerce conversions and enforce its practices. Christianity became the religion of the two swords—the sword of the spirit and the sword of steel. Such tactics were justified by a misapplication of the Scriptures. For example, Luke 22:38, "And they said, Lord, behold here are two swords. And he said unto them, It is enough." Also in Luke 14 after the poor, the maimed, the halt, and the blind are invited to the feast, the servants are told, "Go out into the highways and hedges, and *compel* them to come in" (14:23). By 1150 this formula was so old as to be unquestioned. "Two swords belong to Peter: the one in his hand the other is at his command whenever it is needful to draw it . . . both the material and spiritual sword belong to the church, the latter is drawn for the church, the former by the church. One belongs to the priest and the other to the soldier; but this one is drawn by the orders of the priest."[1]

Those of us who today bask in the sunlight of religious liberty may be shocked at the reminder that the Reformers did not repudiate the state or territorial church concept. Two hundred years later our own founders suffered from the use of the two swords. Even the New England colonists used the secular government to enforce the rules of the church.

The battle cry of the Reformers was, "the just shall live by faith." It marked a return to the Scriptures for the plan of salvation. For this we are indebted to those who led the way back to the New Testament pattern for the structure of the church. Were this volume to deal with the theology of the church as to salvation rather than ecclesiology it would be proper to consider also the matter of sacramental salvation and the reaction against the works which should accompany and follow faith. In the matter of the church, the Reformers, in practice at least, shied away from the New Testament pattern that the Christians constituted a community within a community. To them, the whole community was the church.

Both Luther and Calvin, in spite of the break with Romanism over the authority of the Scriptures versus that of the church, compromised in adopting the concept of the territorial church. Leonard Verduin calls attention to the fact that Luther was faced with a dilemma, the dilemma of wanting both a confessional church based on personal faith and a regional church including all in a given locality:

This dilemma was a cruel one. He who thinks of the Church as a community of experiential believers is bound to oppose him who thinks of it as a fellowship embracing all in a given territory; he who operates with the concept of the church as a society embracing all in a given geographic area must of necessity look askance at the one who restricts the church to the believing ones. The two views cannot be combined; one cancels out the other. In the one view the church is the Corpus Christus, the body of Christ, which consists of believing folk and of them solely; in the other view the church is the Corpus Christianium, the body of a "christened" society. Upon the horns of this dilemma Luther was impaled. And not only Luther—all the rest of the Reformers were torn between the same two alternatives. They, one and all, halted between two opinions. They one and all tried to avoid an outright choice. All tried to ride the fence.[2]

Franklin Hamlin Littell writes of the same failure:

The coming of the Reformation did not bring, in short, any immediate decline of the concept of Corpus Christianium although it introduced more open division into it. Luther and Calvin both thought in terms of complimentary territorial and religious institutions, and both were bitterly opposed to any pluralism of religious communities within a given territory—Zwingli and Calvin both were inspired by the vision of the early church, but shied away from the steps toward a radical restitution.[3]

He concludes that the Reformers, one and all, believed that to maintain discipline in the new-found freedom from Rome it had to be done in the old medieval way through the civil magistrates rather than in any "new" way based on the practices in the time of the earliest church.

Many free church-minded joined Calvin, Luther, Zwingli and the others only to withdraw in bitter disappointment when they realized that the Reformers, though breaking with the establishment in many areas of faith, failed to do so in the territorial concept. These opposed the use of the sword of steel. They did not believe the State should be used as the tool for promoting the Christian church. Luther ridiculed the dissenters accusing them of carrying, not a sword of steel but a *stabler* (little staff)—a harmless staff, or cane, or even a wooden sword as used by children in playing soldiers.

He was not alone in the State Church idea. The Belgic Confession, Article 36, is most revealing (Reformed Churches in America, Holland, and Belgium). The view expressed may no longer reflect the thinking of those confessions today but we are referring to the attitudes at the time of the Reformation.

> We believe that our gracious God because of the depravity of mankind, both appointed kings, princes, and magistrates, willing that the world should be governed by certain laws and policies; to the end that the dissoluteness of men might be restrained, and all things carried on among them with good order and decency. For this purpose, he hath invested the magistracy with the sword, for the punishment of evil doers and for the praise of them that do well. And their office is, not only to have regard unto and watch for the welfare of the civil state, but also that they protect that sacred ministry, and thus may *remove and prevent all idolatry and false worship*; that the kingdom of the antichrist may be thus destroyed, and thist promoted. They must, therefore, countenance the preaching of the Gospel everywhere, that God may be honored and worshiped by everyone, as he commands in his Word.

Those who either withdrew from the Reformers or never joined them in the first place believed that the New Testament teaches that not all men in a given community are or will be Christians in the biblical sense. They believed that the Scriptures reveal society as composed of a diversity of factions. Some will glory in the cross of Christ while others find it offensive. Some will rejoice over the very things of which others may be ashamed. But all can live together peacefully at "the market place without worshiping at the same shrine." Generally, those who held these views were passive. The active, and at times violent, opposition came from the new establishment. The story of the persecution of these believers by the territorial churches makes one of the many dark pages in church history—even more tragic than that of Christians persecuted by the Roman pagans or Protestants by the Roman Catholics. It seems that minorities once they achieve a majority status adopt the tactics of the vanquished majority.

There developed what Verduin[4] calls the men of the Second Front. It became apparent to the Reformers that this front was formidable. The men of the Second Front scorned the use of the sword of steel relying only on the sword of the Spirit forcing the Reformers to divide their forces against Rome and what some called the radicals. Zwingli admitted in a letter to a friend that the struggle with the Catholic party was but "child's play" when compared with the erupting struggle on the Second Front.

Many names were given to those which included the Anabaptists, Mennonites, Herrnhuts, Congregationalists, and others. The dissenter movements in Scandinavia did not develop until about two hundred years later. It was these later groups that Lars Qualben called the *Restorers.*

But it is applicable to the dissenters of the 16th century as well.

> The decline in the moral religious life at the close of the 18th and beginning of the 19th century caused a number of men in America and abroad to locate the trouble in the divided condition of Christendom. As a remedy they proposed to go back of all creeds and councils, of all denominations and schools and what they understood to be the doctrines, ordinances, and practices of primitive Christianity. They aimed to be restorers, not reformers.[5]

The name Radicals was also attached to the men of the Second Front. This is inadequate as it implies that they were similar to but more headlong than the Reformers—that they sought to out-Luther Luther and out-Calvin Calvin. The difference was not quantitative but qualitative. They have also been referred to as the Left Wing of Protestantism. This may be misleading because when it comes to theology they were very much on the right. They were left of the establishment in holding to a living faith rather than a mere assent to a theological system. The name which seems most descriptive to this writer is suggested by Leonard Verduin's book, *The*

Reformers and Their Stepchildren and is used as the heading of this chapter. As he suggests:

> This name is appropriate for two reasons; first because men of the second front were treated as stepchildren allegedly are wont to be treated; second, because they were the victims of a second marriage.[6]

The marriage, of course, is the one uniting the church and the State.

The basic failure of the Reformation, and the one which caused not only the tragedies of the 16th century but the very conflicts which led to the Free Church movements in the 19th century, was that of not searching as diligently in the Scriptures for a polity for the church as they did for the principles of the Christian faith.

The Evangelical Free Church is the result of a sincere attempt at a consistent application of the principles of the Reformation to church polity. Though the Reformers started out rejecting all authority save that of the Holy Scriptures, there were shortcomings in the application of that principle. None of the leading Reformers accepted the necessity of conforming the church polity to the same standard as the doctrine. The importance of the reformation of the doctrine took priority to the extent of bypassing the other entirely. A system of control of the church had to be devised, not on the basis of Scripture, but as a matter of expediency. In the period of transition there was the threat of anarchy now that churches were free from the heavy hand of Rome. Because of this, they put aside whatever concept they might have had in the beginning of the new church and turned to the civil authorities in the various countries for support.

Calvin, for example, while seeking to base his system of church structure on the Word of God, nevertheless compromised for the sake of expediency to cope with the situation at Geneva. He admitted on one occasion at least, that his eldership concept was primarily a device of expediency.[7]

This failure to go all the way is what created the stepchildren. And so there were the two movements—the establishment which recognized every baptized person living in a given territory as a member of the church and the stepchildren who believed that the church was a fellowship of believers. An example of the thinking can be seen in a summary of the teachings of the Anabaptists.[8] They believed that (1) a true church was a company of believers gathered out of the world to which men were admitted by confession and baptism; (2) that each congregation of believers should be independent of all external control, civil or ecclesiastical, and that civil magistrates had no authority over the church; (3) that no believer should bear the sword, take oath, or hold the office of a magistrate; (4) that each congregation should be kept pure by discipline, and should be led by elders chosen by itself, who should serve it without compensation. In the latter, the elders held the role of pastors and not rulers.

Not all of the views of those who followed in the Anabaptist tradition will strike a responsive chord in the minds of those of the Evangelical Free Church position. A brief review will reveal why. Though the spiritual heritage has come from the European continent, primarily Scandinavia, the Free Church ecclesiastical concepts were influenced by what was happening in England following the Reformation and carried over to New England in the United States by the Separatists, Pilgrims, and Puritans. The theme of the influence of American Congregationalism on the polity of the Free Church is one which will be repeatedly stressed in these chapters.

The reformation in England, if it can be called that, was more a matter of a political conflict than a theological one. The Pope was replaced by the King in 1534, seventeen years after the beginning of the Reformation on the continent. There was little other change. The church was a State Church controlled from London instead of Rome. By 1582 the law prohibited any form of worship which was not in agreement with the Church of England. A violation was considered treason against the State and punishable by death. Our forefathers faced similar restrictions two hundred years later. As on the continent, there developed the Second Front which led eventually to the establishment of the Free or Congregational Church.

One of the earliest statements on the principles was drafted in 1582 by Robert Browne (1550-1631). One is tempted to review his hectic life but anyone interested can find much literature on it. He came to the conclusion that the all-inclusive membership of the Church of England was close to being fatal to real piety. He advocated that the only course for those who would seek a full Christian life was to separate from it and form fellowships among themselves. He also believed that local, independent congregations had responsibilities to one another and advocated the "meetings of sundrie churches: which are when the weaker churches seeke helpe of the stronger, for deciding or redressing of matters or else the stronger look to them for redresse."[9]

A summary of his position for comparison and in contrast to that of the Anabaptists will give evidence as to one source of the thinking of our founders. He believed (1) that it was the duty of Christians to separate from communions where non-Christians were tolerated; (2) that the magistrate had no right to coerce men's consciences; (3) that a local congregation was to be independent with the right to choose its own officers, exercise its own discipline. On the other hand, (4) he rejected the tenet of believers baptism; (5) declared that oaths were sometimes not only lawful but a special furtherance of the Kingdom of God; (6) held that there was nothing unbecoming in a Christian holding civil office; (7) and that a Christian should not hesitate to bear arms.[10]

One of the historians summarized the contribution of Browne and the other leaders on the Second Front. While admitting that the details were not fully developed and that people like Browne did not pretend to speak for others, they did make definite contributions toward applying the principles of the Reformation to church polity. "It steered a safe course between the sacrifice of self-government of the local church for the sake of a strong central authority which is the evil feature of all systems from Romanism to Presbyterianism, and the abandonment of real mutual accountability between churches which had been the vulnerable point of the polity of the Anabaptist."[11]

In the eyes of the stepchildren, there was also another shortcoming on the part of the Reformers. The Word of God should provide not only the basis for doctrine and polity but for a way of life. This led to Pietism, a movement which started in the Lutheran Church of Germany in the 17th century and laid stress on a life of devotion to Christ. This movement spread to Scandinavia and prepared the way for the spiritual revivals of the last century. The lifestyle of the Free Church founders reflected pietism.

The reaction to the territorial church concept did not really become a force in Scandinavia until the 1800s which in turn resulted in the Free Movement. This brings us to 1884. The immigrants involved came to America the latter half of the 1800s. The revivals in the countries from which they came and the similar revivals in the new country in which they had now settled created a dilemma. In breaking away from the State Churches and finding a new religious freedom in America, what should the believers do about organizing a local church? What should be the relationship of one church to another? What does the Word of God teach? Is not there a biblical pattern for the polity of a church as well as for doctrinal principles? Has not history proven this to be the case? But must we not reconcile that history and the conclusions of those who faced this question two centuries before we were forced to face it? In the persecution of the believers in Scandinavia in the nineteenth century we see history repeating itself. But must we merely accept the patterns of those who broke with the Reformers in the beginning without searching the Scriptures—comparing the polity of those movements with what stands written? In the freedom of our new nation we have the opportunity to study carefully, discuss openly, and build our church on the foundation of the apostles and prophets and all the believers who have followed, with Jesus Christ as the Head of the corner. To this task our founders gave themselves.

FOOTNOTES—CHAPTER I

1. Verduin, Leonard, *The Reformers and Their Stepchildren*, Wm. B. Eerdmans Publishing Co., Grand Rapids, 1964. p. 43
2. *Ibid*, p. 17
3. Littell, Franklin, *The Free Church*, Star King Press, Boston 1957, p. 17
4. Verduin, op. cit., p. 13
5. Qualben, Lars, *A History of the Christian Church*, Thomas Nelson and Sons, 1939, p. 566
6. Verduin, op. cit., p. 13
7. Dexter, H. M., *Congregationalism of the Last Three Hundred Years as Seen in its Literature*, New York, 1880, p. 52, 53 as quoted by Williston Walker
8. Walker, Williston, *The Creeds and Platforms of Congregationalism*, Pilgrim Press, Boston, 1893, p. 3
9. *Ibid*, p. 14
10. In other words, they did not hold to rebaptism, a charge made against the Anabaptist. The Free Church position will be discussed in another volume.
11. Walker, Williston, op. cit., p. 17

Chapter II
THE SEARCH BEGINS

Biblical exegesis does not necessarily become more accurate with time. The founders of the Evangelical Free Church were dedicated to basing the principles and policies of the new church as well as the doctrine on the Scriptures. The challenge of those early days was, *Huru staar det skrevet?* (How stands it written?)[1] They searched the New Testament for the blueprint. Contrary to what some may assume, the men and women providing the leadership in this task were well trained in ecclesiology. They knew the church structures of that day. In fact, they were a century closer to the days of the Reformation and the debates, controversies and personalities which had led to the development of the main forms of church organization—the episcopal, presbyterian and congregational.

The search was long and the struggles toward a conclusion difficult. Not only was it the matter of understanding the Scriptures and being steeped in church history but the task of uniting leaders who had suffered much at the hands of the religious establishment. That trauma resulted in fears and suspicions which needed to be overcome. The experiences had created a generation of strong-willed individuals which proved a mixed blessing.

Their conclusions did not exclude all other forms of

church structure. They recognized the fact that the New Testament has not given us a clear, simple pattern and that others might be equally sincere in building a different type of church also based on what they considered a Biblical pattern. However, our pioneers came to the conclusion that the congregational system came closest to what they understood the New Testament to prescribe. It lays stress on the fellowship of believers and the priesthood of everyone as the foundation for forming the local congregation and the larger fellowship. The position of pastor is not so much one of authority but of a leader, teacher and under-shepherd.

How did they reach such a choice? That is the purpose of this study. We must begin with the great horde of immigrants who came to America during the last half of the 19th century. They did not come to this new land motivated above all else by a longing for religious freedom. By the time we reach the 1870s many of the restrictions and the conventicle laws had been rescinded.[2] They emigrated for economic and political reasons. True, some had already been converted in the spiritual revivals moving across the Scandinavian countries but even they came for economic reasons. Few of them had actually broken openly with the State Church. Even today some members of the Free Evangelical Churches of Europe, belonging to the International Federation[3], hold a dual membership. In six countries the members have left the State Churches while in the other six the matter is optional.[4]

On reaching America, the influences of childhood and youth was in evidence as the immigrants gravitated to the Swedish, Norwegian and Danish Lutheran churches which were the counterpart of the State Churches at home. Some attended out of sheer loneliness in the new country. At church they would feel at home in familiar surroundings, meet other newcomers, some from their old villages, and communicate in the mother tongue. Many were also discouraged. The streets of the new land were not paved with gold nor had they reached the end of the rainbow. In spite of these setbacks, the immigrant loved his new land and lived in hope for his children and grandchildren.

It was also a time of great spiritual revivals. Many of the immigrants were ripe for such an awakening and were converted. Following the practice in the old country, they formed prayer and Bible study groups without severing connections with the Lutheran bodies. They needed the services of the established church—for marriage, the baptism of their children, a place for burial, etc. There was the familiar cycle—a mission society within the church—an independent society outside the church—but still not a separate organized congregation. As these new believers grew in the knowledge of the Scriptures they began to react against the teachings, structure, liturgy and the clerical dictatorship.

However, the concept of an organized congregation entirely apart from the establishment meeting all the needs of the new believers developed slowly. In Europe there were the restrictions of the State Churches. In America, supposedly a land of religious freedom, the pioneers began to rebel against the repressive inconsistencies of the established churches. The Lutheran bodies, against which they reacted, held to the need for a rebirth through church membership communicated by acts of the church. But they had been brought up in the church and though supposedly born again since their baptism as infants they were not saved. The new believers held to the new birth as the result of a personal, conscious act of repentance for sin and a commitment to Christ as Savior and Lord. Further, they could no longer accept communion together with unbelievers as it was the Lord's table prepared for the Lord's people.

E. A. Halleen observes that the situation was somewhat similar to that of one who has come out of prison:

> Life had been cut and dried, everything prescribed. Their going in and coming out had been strictly regulated from some headquarters. In this new country and with a new environ-

ment they developed new qualities. They became individualists. They refused to "lock up" with the masses, like one soldier keeping step with a million other men, doing what others were doing and not because they wanted to do it. The pioneers had no aspiration to become so many grains of sand in the vast desert; a few drops of water in the wide, wide sea. They wanted to be free men and women.

Christ had made them free. Free to think for themselves. Free to develop this sacred trust of thought and will. There were outward circumstances that contributed to this also. Great numbers of our pioneers settled in sparsely occupied communities. Miles of unbroken soil lay between them and their nearest neighbor. Even the cities and towns were loosely built and organized. An unhampered freedom reigned everywhere—freedom and great possibilities.[5]

There was also the industrial revolution which was taking place in America in the latter half of the last century.

Karl Olsson, the gifted historian of the Evangelical Covenant Church, in a paper read to the Theological Conference of delegates from the denominations in the International Federation of Free Evangelical Churches related this revolution to the beginnings of the two denominations in America.[6]

The decade of 1881-1890 which saw the birth of both the Evangelical Free Church and the Evangelical Covenant Church was much like our present time, a seething caldron. It was a time which heralded change for the sake of change and in part at least dared to question the established sanctities.

The proletariat about which Marx and Engels had written learnedly in the 1850s and 60s became in the 1880s a significant social force. Communists, socialists, anarchists not only preached their disturbing gospel; they demonstrated, they marched, they struck.

He continues that there developed

The new self consciousness of the working man, his discovery of the bitterness which lived inside his skull, his toying with violence as a fast, effective means of asserting his identity and his right to be and to decide over his own destiny.

After comparing the conditions then with those existing now in the struggle for human rights, he concludes:

> It is impossible to understand the development of the Evangelical Free Church and the Evangelical Covenant Church without seeing them in this larger social context. Both bodies resulted from action and reaction. They were the products of powerful new forces in history and the emergence of the creative work of the Holy Spirit, but they were also in reaction to the stultifying of the influences of the religious establishments.
>
> There was in the 1880s a radicalizing of attitudes. This was the decade of the great Ibsen plays with their attacks on any society which presumes to inhibit the development of the individual. Ibsen, we recall, was not, as he is sometimes presented, a social prophet, but a radical individualist who saw love and freedom as the only cement between persons.[7] The eighties also saw the publication of some of August Strindberg's most powerful plays, these also attack the tyranny which society exercises over individuals.

In this, he supports the observation made by Halleen as quoted previously. The break took two forms. Some left the established churches quietly and individually. In other places, large numbers withdrew at one time in the midst of much controversy and emotion. In the smaller communities there were attempts at social ostracism and economic boycotts by the established and dominating church in the community.

This was the situation in the town of the first church I later had the privilege of serving as pastor.[8] Tent meetings were conducted among the members of the local Lutheran Church creating great animosity. It divided families; neighbors; in fact, the whole town. One act of opposition was the hanging of a stretched, bleeding pig outside the tent during a service in protest against the preacher's constant emphasis on the cleansing power of the shed blood of Christ. Another incident, verified by my own conversations with the men involved, was the visit by two members of the church at the suggestion of the pastor. While both men were drunk he implanted the idea that in that state they would break up the meeting. Sitting in the first row, directly in front of the evangelist, they themselves became deeply disturbed under the convicting power of the Holy Spirit and ended up at the altar calling upon God for forgiveness. They became instantly sobered as the evangelist spoke! Both men became trophies of the transforming power of the Gospel and not only leaders in the new local fellowship but in the denomination as well. The entire town witnessed a radical change. I recall during my pastorate how the president of the bank, whose son was a Roman Catholic Bishop, invited one of these men to visit him, read the Scriptures and pray during what became his final illness (no other visitors were allowed). For over forty years this man, like many others, gave daily evidence of his conversion.

On the other hand, some of those who formed the core of these new fellowships had already made a break with the religious establishment in the old countries. Though these had not withdrawn their membership, they did not seek affiliation with the counterparts of the State Churches on arrival in America. Most of them came following 1878 from Sweden and 1884 from Norway when the Mission Covenants had been formed in those countries, respectively.[9] They had already tasted the new fellowship after their conversion in the revivals that spawned the local assemblies, which in turn became parts of the new dissenter denominations.

My parents were of that group. My father, faithful in his attendance at the "Høi Messe" (High Mass) on Sunday morning in the State Church, would attend a prayer and Bible study in a prayer house (Bede Hus) in the afternoon where he accepted Christ as Savior and Lord. This was in a small Norwegian town on the Swedish border. My mother was converted, as a very young girl, during one of Norway's most enduring revivals in the mountain country of southern Norway. Both emigrated to America and settled temporarily in northern Minnesota where they met

26

while attending a Swedish Mission Church. On moving to Minneapolis they were married and attended the Swedish Free Church until the Norwegian Evangelical Free Church was organized and remained as charter members of that church until their final emigration to a far better land.

Had they not met with the free movements in Norway and sensed an indebtedness to those who brought them the Gospel, it is doubtful they would have, in the beginning at least, sought fellowship outside the State Church counterpart. In that case, it is doubtful that they might have met each other and I may never have been born!

But the great majority of the immigrants who eventually became the members of the Evangelical Free Churches were converted during the great revivals of those days after coming to the American shores.

The need for fellowship with people speaking the same Scandinavian language, believers with like precious faith and similar experiences was almost immediately felt. As these new groups grew in number they faced the problems of adequate meeting places, buying land, erecting buildings, starting cemeteries, and granting authorization to leaders who could perform, on behalf of the State, certain duties such as marriage. This raised the question of ordination, a problem they had not had to face in the old country nor in America as long as they were affiliated with an established church, usually like the State Church. There were two pressures forcing them, though often reluctantly, to incorporate. The first was the need already mentioned and the second was that to function legally they had to incorporate no matter how "worldly" it seemed to some. They were to function not only under the Lordship of Christ but also the laws of the State. If they were to organize locally, what kind of organization was in accordance with the Scriptures? Is it possible to have a New Testament church in a secular society? Is it possible to commit ourselves to an organization which meets state laws as a secular corporation without compromising our commitment to the Head of the Church? Is it possible to design a structure which guarantees the newly-found liberty in the Holy Spirit? Is it possible to create an ordained clergy who will be the servants, not the masters, of the congregation? Is it possible to stay clear of adopting a restrictive creedal position which could divide us after the unity we have enjoyed since we were born again? On the other hand, is it possible to maintain the purity of doctrine without submitting ourselves to a narrowly definitive doctrinal statement?

By the time we reach the year 1884 many of their questions were answered satisfactorily resulting in a number of duly organized congregations—some belonging to either the Mission or Ansgar Synod, about which we will report later, or remaining independent. The question of local organizations gave way to a larger and more difficult one.

Halleen, though he was not on the scene as early as 1884, lived close enough to the emotions of those days to articulate them with a contagious enthusiasm:[10]

> Revivals swept over many states and communities in the early days of our work. Those saved in the homeland were now wondrously revived. Others were wondrously saved. It was a time of great upheaval and joy. The joy note of the redeemed was simply exuberant. Nothing less will describe it. And true joy is an expression of inner freedom—a freedom that can be enjoyed under cramped exterior boundaries, but which seemed to have reached its highest pinnacle in the promising environment of the new country.

> With this new experience of revival and salvation came the need for fellowship. The thing that happened was too big and too good to keep to oneself. Men and women, learned and unlearned, found themselves compelled to go out and tell it to others. Shoemakers, harnessmakers, teachers and doctors became preachers overnight. Like Amos the prophet, they were called from the sheep cote or other places of business or employment, to go out with the Gospel. And none of us who went out could say we came with the fullness of the Gospel of Christ. We did not know the Bible very well, nor did we know much of Him of whom the Bible speaks. Our knowledge was fragmentary but our hearts were full, and "out of the abun-

dance of the heart, the mouth speaketh."[11]

The leaders within our church were in the beginning mostly evangelists. God used them mightily in soul winning. Let it be said that this is still the characteristic of o' r work and for that we are indeed thankful.[12]

But there was also what he called "the aversion to organizations, to rules and regulations which found its most fertile soil relative to the national work." Hence it took several years before the actual organization took place.

This was the period of the search—the search for identity. If we must have a national organization will it help to carry out the great commission? If we do organize as an Association of Congregations, a National Fellowship of Independent Churches, a denomination or what have you, shall it be episcopal in its structure—governed by an individual; presbyterian—governed by a committee be it a board of elders, a presbytery, or a classis either on the local, district or national level; or congregational—in which each local congregation is autonomous in all local church matters and where decisions are made by the united group or made by the representatives of those churches?

Adding to the problem was the fact that the Scriptures do not spell out in detail a pattern for a local church structure or inter-church relations. In the introduction we have sought to summarize the conclusions of the founders as they saw it in the Bible. Some today, who would say, "we follow the Bible and not Free Church tradition" need to remember three facts. First, the founders had no traditions of their own. They were about to blaze new trails among the Scandinavians as far as church polity was concerned. Second, the emphasis in the early days was on the Bible—how was it written? Third, the fact that there were already three major types of church structure accepted by people whose founders had been equally sincere, scholarly, and determined to have a church after a New Testament pattern gives additional proof that no group could really say they followed the Word of God and the others

29

did not.

Even when today we speak of the Free Church tradition it does not mean that it is in contradiction to the Scriptures. Not all traditions are bad. One must find whether or not they are the kind of traditions of men which Paul condemns (Col. 2:8) or those traditions which he commends, "Therefore, brethren, stand fast, and hold the traditions which ye have been taught, whether by word or our epistle" (II Thess. 2:15). Church structures are not mutually exclusive to those who recognize these facts, as did our fathers. Without claiming a monopoly on the right structure, they concluded that the identity upon which they finally agreed came the closest in their study to what the New Testament taught. As we come to the final chapter, we will see the respect they held for the other views without compromising their own.

An open-minded study of church polity as revealed in the practices of the New Testament may well lead one through an evolution of opinions. Lest the author appear subjective, he finds it wise to suggest the conclusions of one who was on the faculty of the Chicago Theological Seminary at the beginning and later the first president of North Park College, David Nyvall.

> Under what we have called the constitution of the New Testament the apostolic execution of their commission has a history starting in Jerusalem with democracy under the regime of Peter, modified later in Jerusalem under James, as in Galatia, Macedonia, and Hellas under Paul into presbyterianism of a sort, ending in Asia with a complete episcopacy under Paul and John. On these simple facts are based all the warning claims for the rule of one as the permanent form of church government. Those in favor of popular government, the Congregationalists prove to their own satisfaction that this form of government certainly was the first choice, the first love to which we better return. Those who favor class rule, the Presbyterians, whether Lutherans or Calvinists, prove to their own satisfaction that this form of government, the government by experts, was the mature choice of the apostles in Jerusalem and therefore an abiding climax of perfection which we had better follow. Those who favor the one man's

power, the Episcopalians, prove to their own satisfaction that this form of government is the grand climax of enlightened apostolic wisdom and human experience, abundantly proving its supreme value by its success.[13]

These were the options already available to the pioneers. If there were others, they certainly would also have been in existence after 1800 years of church history. It is this search which will be considered in the remaining chapters. The decision as to the type of structure ranked second to the question, why have one at all? It was to the people of that time a most formidable task and to us a challenge to preserve and enhance the heritage of that which came out of the prayers, the study of the Word, and the eventual consensus of our forefathers.

Footnotes—Chapter II

1. Paul Peter Waldenstrom, 1838-1917, a theologian, scholar and spiritual leader in Sweden, may well be called the founder of the Missions Forbund (Mission Covenant of Sweden). His name appears in two segments of this volume. He was, at the beginning, an ordained minister of the State Church. David Nyvall (see Chapter III) writes that his two major contributions to the movement and among the Swedish mission people in America were his insistence on going directly to the Word of God for doctrinal truth—How stands it written?—and his insistence that salvation comes through a personal and subjective commitment to Jesus Christ as Savior and Lord and not through the mediation of the church.
2. Conventicles. A law prohibiting any religious gathering, even by members of the State Church, outside the church and apart from the control of the church clergy.
3. The International Federation was organized in 1948. Plans were well under way earlier but interrupted during World War II.
4. The denominations belonging are those in Finland (two—the Swedish Mission Church of Finland in the south and the Finnish Mission Church in the north), Sweden, Norway, Denmark, Germany, Holland, Belgium, France, Czechoslovakia, Spain, Greece, the United States (two) and Canada (one).
5. Halleen, E. A., *Sunshine and Shadows*, 1944, published by the *Evangelical Beacon*, p. 167.
6. The Conference was held at Trinity Evangelical Divinity School and North Park Seminary in 1971.
7. Ibsen was a young man at the time of the LAMMERS Revival in the middle of the nineteenth century. Lammers, who was a pastor in the State Church, left and championed the right of believers to leave the State Church and form independent congregations. Many joined him. Ibsen's sister joined the Lammers movement; his mother attended the services; and his youngest brother,

31

a man of deep religious convictions, was recognized as a member of the free congregation. It is believed that one of Ibsen's characters in Brand was based on Lammers. He has been quoted as saying to Henrik Jaeger that Kierkegaard was too much of a lecture hall agitator while Lammers was an outdoor soap box agitator as is BRAND (Lammers, upon his expulsion from the church, preached in the village square.)

8. The writer served the congregation at Houston, Minnesota, 1930-33. The evangelist was Christian Oftedal, supported by the Home Mission Society of the American Congregational Church.

9. In Scandinavia the denominations are called Missions Forbund (Mission Union or Covenant Association) while the similar denominations in America are called the Evangelical Covenant and Evangelical Free Church. The Covenant of Sweden has close ties with the one in America while the Free Church, because of the old Norwegian-Danish Free Church, still maintains ties with those in Norway and Denmark. For a history of the Federation and the member denominations see the book *Believers Only.*

10. *Sunshine and Shadows,* p. 169.

11. Chapter III will reveal that there were also in leadership a number of well-educated churchmen.

12. This was written in 1944. We might wonder if he could say the same 35 years later!

13. Nyvall, David, *The Evangelical Covenant Church,* Covenant Press, Chicago, 1954, p. 108, First published under the title, the Swedish Covenanters in 1929.

CHAPTER III

BUT THERE WERE OBSTACLES

As a lad growing up in Minneapolis, I traveled every Sunday by trolley through the church history of the Swedish believers without realizing it. We lived at the time in the north section of the city while our church, a Norwegian-Danish Evangelical Free Church, was on the southside, necessitating a thirty-minute streetcar ride. The car passed by six churches, all on the same street, each representing one of the Swedish congregations dating as far back as 1884. On the first corner was the Swedish Tabernacle, now the First Covenant Church. Two blocks farther stood the Swedish Temple, the house of the Independents (Frias), now the Central Free Church. In the same block but on the next corner was the Swedish (Augustana Synod) Lutheran Church. One block farther on we'd pass by the Swedish Evangelical Free Church, now the First Church and located elsewhere. Another block farther and one saw the Swedish Baptist Church, now the Bethlehem Baptist. Had I been born a decade earlier, I would also have passed the Swedish Methodist Church across from the Baptists.[1]

These were the options open to the founders. Why not take the easy way? If they did not want to stay in the

Augustana Synod, why not join the Baptists or Methodists? Or better still, why not wait until 1885 and join the other churches planning to become members of the anticipated formation of what today is known as The Evangelical Covenant Church? Or, if they were so afraid of denominationalism, why not decide to become or remain independent congregations like the one worshipping in the Swedish Temple?

The matter of whether or not a local church should be organized had been quite well settled by the time we reached the 1884-1885 period. If that were not the case there would have been no need for the search for identity. Had there been no congregations there could have been no meetings to discuss what they could do together to carry out the Lord's Commission to the Church and how they might unite to do so without jeopardizing the independence of the participating congregations.

But there were many obstacles in the way to even engaging seriously in the search. Without some knowledge of these, those who have become familiar with the principles and polity of the denomination, as they finally developed, will have difficulty understanding the churches and the church at large.

The first obstacle would be the memories of experiences under the State Churches of the Scandinavian countries. We are not discussing the theology of the Church but rather the practices. Many believers were persecuted, leaders were imprisoned, restrictions applied. Would some of the same control be exercised even in a country granting full religious freedom? Impossible, you say? Some had already experienced opposition, not from the State but from the churches which were the counterparts of those in Scandinavia.

Let's take a brief look at developments in the countries from which the founders had come. The three major controversies during the last century were the right to free assembly outside and apart from the church, the right to hold communion services apart from the church and served by one who may or may not have been an ordained priest of the church, and the right to have infants baptized by laymen and still have the birth registered in the records of the parish church. The last issue was not a matter of the time and mode of baptism. That was a controversy between them and the State as represented by the State Churches. Both Norway and Sweden had laws prohibiting assembly for religious purposes outside the church and apart from the leadership of the church. In Norway it was ordered in 1741 and lifted in 1842 while in Sweden it was in effect from 1726 to 1858.

One cannot study this period without reading of Hans Neilsen Hauge. Converted in 1796, he felt moved, as a layman, to preach the Gospel to his fellow Norwegians. So important was the day of his conversion (April 5th), that historians have called the date as the one marking the turning point in church history—the day the old order ended and the new one began. From 1797 to 1804 revival fires were kindled wherever he traveled resulting in the violent opposition of the clergy. In 1798 alone he was beaten three times and imprisoned three times. A number of his followers were also imprisoned. The next year Hauge was placed in prison where he languished for nine years before being brought to trial. Released temporarily in 1811 he was finally sentenced in 1814 to two years at hard labor. It was a bishop of the church who had him arrested and charged with (a) a violation of the law against free assembly, (b) attacking the Lutheran priests for turning from revelation through Scriptures to rationalism, and (c) leading peasants to a state of religious exaggeration and fanatacism. In spite of the persecution he remained loyal to the church and called upon his followers in his last will and testament to do the same. He did, however, sow the seed for a free movement by (a) introducing the idea that a fellowship of believers was the true congregation, (b) that local leaders chosen by the people themselves should be responsible for church discipline, and (c) lay persons had the right to assemble and to preach.

The next phase took place following what is known as the Lammers Revival (Adolph Gustav Lammers, 1802-1878). He went beyond Hauge, broke with the church, deplored the practice of serving the Lord's Supper to believers and non-believers alike and supported the right of believers to withdraw from the Lutheran Church and establish local independent congregations.[2]

The rebellion in Sweden followed similar but more readily defined stages. The opposition to the right of assembly and the right of non-State Church preachers were equally violent. For example, a Methodist missionary, George Scott from London, was the instrument of a revival in Stockholm in the 1830s. So great was the opposition of the clergy that on Palm Sunday in 1842 a mob attacked him breaking up the meeting and forcing him out of Sweden ten days later.[3] Swedish leaders such as Carl Olaf Rosenius (1816-1868), a giant in the early revival movement, was profoundly stirred by the treatment of Scott. Following the tragic events during the Scott revival, Rosenius initiated mission meetings and promoted prayer and Bible study gatherings apart from and in defiance of the laws against assembly. The second giant was Paul Peter Waldenstrom (1838-1917) who is generally recognized as the founder of the Mission Church in Sweden. Though a duly ordained minister in the State Church, he also defied the church. Eventually the governments both in Norway and Sweden were pressured into repealing the Conventicle Law.

Next came the battle over the right to hold communion apart from the State Church. In Sweden in 1877, a committee brought a petition to the King bearing 22,300 signatures requesting that (a) the observance of Holy Communion be made unrestricted as the preaching of the Divine Word now is, (b) in consequence, such stipulations of the Church Laws be removed which make it criminal for Lutheran Christians, urged by their consciences, to exercise that freedom which both the Word of Christ as well as the words of Luther afford them.

The petition was rejected by the King and so the mission societies went underground and formed Secret Sacramental Societies. This was not unique to Sweden. It was also the experience of other congregations throughout Europe. The catalyst in most instances was not a controversy over baptism, as some suppose, but over who should partake and who should serve communion. It was this denial of freedom which became the "last straw" leading to the formation of the Swedish Mission Church a year later.

There remained another hurdle in the path to religious freedom. Infant baptism was the means by which a person's birth was duly registered. The names were not kept in the courthouse but in the local church. The rite had to be performed by a priest of the church. Believers did not object to the baptism of their children as there was no alternative to having a birth recognized as legitimate but they objected to it being done by an unregenerate priest in the name of a religion in which he may not believe and much less practice.

In 1860 a father baptized his own child only to find the priest would not rebaptize the infant for the sake of registering the birth. In 1880 another layman was arrested for a similar act and charged with assuming the role of a priest. The case went to the highest court which ruled that the name of the child could be registered providing the notation was added after the name, date of birth, etc.; namely, "by a layman." In June of 1896 a royal degree supported the decision of the court. This aroused the clergy to the extent that 1,697 of them petitioned the crown to withdraw the approval. Months of debate followed, including a visit to the King by Waldenstrom. The King turned to the Council of Bishops who advised that laymen could baptize and that the name should thus be entered in the church records but that the words "not by the Church of Sweden" rather than "by a layman" be added. Apparently a negative statement declaring what had not been done was more satisfactory to the clergy than a positive one![4]

It was during the second half of the nineteenth century that these controversies raged. This adds to our understanding of the desire for independence from a religious establishment. It was also during this half a century that great numbers of Scandinavians emigrated with memories of the oppression fresh in the minds of believers and non-believers.

The second obstacle in the way of deciding upon an organization of local free and independent mission societies was distrust of the clergy system. The movement had been essentially a laymen's movement. This was due in part to the fact that only the Church could ordain and second, that there was freedom in the new groups to study, share and teach the Scriptures. All had equal opportunities though not necessarily equal ability or equal equipment developed through education.

As Karl Olsson observes in the paper introduced in the previous chapter:

> The rejection of the Lutheran patterns was not only a matter of content. It was the repudiation of the notion that doctrine is something developed by the church and imposed on its constituency. Waldenstrom's battle with the church on the atonement issue was also a battle for the right of every Christian to be his own theologian. And the final rejection of the binding effect of the three classical creeds of Christendom as well as of the Lutheran symbola and the placing of the Scriptures as the only rule for faith, doctrine, and conduct was not only a hacking away of the archaic bonds of the church but an affirmation of the primacy of the individual over every establishment, however venerable. It is thus part and parcel of the same *geist* which motivated Ibsen to write *The Enemy of the People*.

> The guardians of the doctrine in the Lutheran churches were the clergy, selected, trained, validated, marshalled, and disciplined by the establishment. The new freedom of the Mission Friends encouraged them to laicize the clergy and to make their primary function preaching, not bearing rule in the church.

They were afraid of a clericized ministry. They were also afraid of a churchly church. To begin with, they had been mission societies within the Augustana churches. Then they became independent societies, then congregations of sorts. Finally, under some pressure from the situation they were pushed in the direction of forming new synods: The Mission Synod in 1873, and the Ansgar Synod a year later. Both Synods, though struggling with the problems of the new life, were formally committed to the old creeds.

This brings us back to the question raised at the beginning of this chapter. There were several options open—the Lutheran, Baptist, Methodist and Independents. Now, in addition to these, there were other possibilities.

Before finding the answer, it is necessary to take a brief look at three synods. The Augustana Lutheran Synod (1868) served as the counterpart to the State Church of Sweden. However, this did not long satisfy those influenced by the revivals, especially in the open membership of the church and the position on the sacraments. The Evangelical Lutheran Mission Synod (1873) was patterned after the free groups though it was Lutheran in its name as well as in doctrine and still tied to Augustana. The Evangelical Lutheran Ansgar Synod (1874) had in its beginning even stronger ties to the Augustana Church.[5] There was neither unity nor uniformity as each had a stormy history in which strong personalities constantly clashed with one another. In 1878 a union of the two synods was proposed. Finally, in August 1884, delegates to a conference of the Ansgar Synod voted to disband while the Mission Synod, though it really never formally disbanded, provided a number of congregations for what would become the Covenant Church. Some of the leaders of the Ansgar Synod became the leaders in the move to form what would eventually become the Swedish Evangelical Free Church composed initially of congregations out of the Ansgar Synod and the Independents.

Why could not the two synods merge into one fellowship entirely apart from the Lutheran influence? There was little, if any, difference in doctrine. However, there was, what seemed to the founders of both the Covenant and Free Church, a wide division when it came to the structure of the national body. The one called for an organization of member churches and the other a fellowship of delegates and ministers from participating churches. Looking back, one might wonder what the difference really was.

Some might be surprised at the thought of becoming a part of the other Swedish denominations represented by the churches on Seventh Street. We must keep the purpose of this volume in mind and primarily the story of the search for a pattern for organization which finally crystallized. We must also take into consideration the period of time which leads up to 1884 and follows immediately after. These groups were not as divided theologically then as they may seem now. It was the structure of a national church which divided them. The Methodists, for example, were ruled by bishops—an unpopular name and role among Free Church families. The Baptists would limit baptism to the immersion of believers and while that would not be offensive, the limitations to one time and form would be a violation of the freedom the Free people considered so important.

If in the search for identity none of the above are acceptable, why not become part of some other denomination already in existence in America or at least follow their pattern of organization—the Presbyterian or Reformed, the Anglican or Episcopalian, or the Congregational. There was first of all a very practical problem, that of language, since Swedish, Norwegian and Danish continued to be the languages of the church well into the twentieth century. Was that not one of the reasons for the existence of churches—to minister to the immigrants and to evangelize those who could best be reached in the mother tongue?

They saw in the presbyterian and reformed a threat to the idea of independence of the members of the local church under the elder system and the dominance of a national body over the member churches. There was also, as in the baptist churches because of the Reformed or Calvinistic theology, a threat to the concept of theological freedom.

The fear of control by a few over the many in a local church was also a deep-seated emotion. Halleen writes of an attempt by a few to exercise such control even apart from holding offices when he assumed the pastorate in Minneapolis.[6]

> Several dwarfed characters had found lodgement in the church who imagined themselves divinely appointed custodians of the mysteries of God in the church. When it became evident that the new pastor did not intend to take dictation from them, everything possible was done to disturb the meetings and to hinder the work. One went so far that he brought suit on two occasions against the pastor. All of these were brands from the emotional fires of the past. This caused no little confusion. However, the church had men of varied experience and of sterling character, and these stood wholeheartedly by me.

This was not an unusual situation in the early days. The loose organization, sometimes without a membership roll, the itinerant preachers who ministered, the right of each to teach the Word as he or she saw it without a structural pattern or doctrinal framework encouraged some to "take over." But to organize and grant official status to a small group? No, never!

A pastor, impatient with the congregation for being slow to follow his leadership and accept his plans for the church, might have wished, at times, he could have been able to control through a board of elders who might bypass the congregation. Even Halleen admitted this. In an address to a general conference over fifty years ago, he said:

> Our polity can be summed up in one word, and that is independence. I have not always liked it. I have felt at times that we should get better control of our people, but it has been rather hard to get. Our people generally found their "authority" when they were facing the looking glass. I do not see any

use of trying to correct this. For fifty years we have been independent and we do not dare use the word "affiliated" in our constitutions. The local independent churches merely "cooperate" in our united enterprises.

Several of the earliest congregations made provisions for elders in their constitution. A typical case would be the one at Denver, founded in 1880. The elders were elected only for the purpose of assisting the pastor in visiting the sick, presiding in the pastor's absence, etc. In other churches that role was given to the deacons. But, in none of the churches in the beginning was there the presbyterian form of local church government. Whether one is under the domination of a bishop, a duly elected board of elders, a self-appointed group, or a pastor-chosen clique, the result is the same as Philip Schaff observed, "Independents have a right to protest against tyranny, whether exercised by bishops or presbyters; for there are *Lord Brethren* as well as *Lord Bishops*.[7]

When it came to a national organization the founders, trained in the seminaries of that day, knew of the failure to unite the congregational and presbyterian concepts. There were a number of attempts to unite the two, both in England and in New England, but all failed and the reasons were proof that one cannot mix iron with clay. For example, in England there was a plan in 1691. One historian noted:

Alike in doctrine, in their hatred of prelacy, and in their conceptions of the proper forms of worship, and largely accordant in their views as to the nature of the ministry and its functions, their great point of divergence was in regard to the existence or non-existence of a national church. To such an institution the Presbyterians clung. In their estimation the local congregation was to be part of a reformed church of England, responsible to a series of church courts which should knit together the whole. In the Congregational view, on the other hand, no such thing as a national church existed. There should be churches each independent, bound to its neighbors by fellowship and advice; but over these churches the Congregationalist would place no ecclesiastical body, self-constituted or representative of the churches as a whole, whose behests could bind the smallest local congregation. Here, then, was a radical and, as experience proved, irreconcilable difference of conception.[8]

In America, there was for a long time a program by which presbyterian pastors would serve a congregational church and the congregational minister, a presbyterian church. One can imagine the conflicts. The presbyterian was not under the discipline of the church he served but under the presbyterian and the congregational under whatever little discipline there was in the ministerial association to which he may have belonged. A man from a creedal church would thus serve a non-creedal congregation and vice-versa. Needless to say, this also failed and after a long period of trial and error the Congregationalists finally, at about the time our founders were contemplating forms of a national association, came out with a national platform and creed.

It was a conflict between whether or not the whole is greater than its parts or the parts, which create the whole, are the greater. This might be as good a place as any to make a confession. I have always held that the parts were not only greater but in agreement with the view just noted by the historian, that there is no such thing as a national church. I have therefore been in many situations where I regretted that at the time of the merger in 1950, when the moment was opportune, I did not write into the plan the name Evangelical Free Churches of America instead of simply adapting the traditional and more readily acceptable at the time, the Evangelical Free Church. The former more clearly declares our attitude towards denominationalism. So I add my confession to the one made by Halleen, quoted earlier, and conclude, as he did, ''I do not see any use of trying to correct this.''

Another obstacle was in the area of semantics. The word denomination was a word which did not really have a literal counterpart in the Scandinavian. The early free church people related it to a system rather than an identification. To them, the very word meant something sinister, something dictatorial, something akin to the State Church concept.

So strong was the feeling that a few of the oldest congregations have written into their constitutions that the church cannot at any time join a denomination. To this day one hears the expression, "But we are not a denomination, we are an association—a fellowship!" The question in 1884 to 1910 was, "How can we work together without becoming a denomination?" A look into an American dictionary would have solved the problem. The summary among the many similar definitions is this: "A group of congregations held together by a common denominator." The denominator may be a creed, a polity, or a purpose. One might say that in the beginning the common denominator among us was independence! As the search for identity succeeded, the common denominator became as follows: "The salvation of souls and the edification of the believers in faith, hope and love by organizing churches, maintaining missionary work at home and abroad, establishing schools, publishing literature to unite churches for mutual efforts in those activities beyond the scope and ability of a local congregation." It took a long time before this was understood.

The final obstacle to overcome in the search for identity was the strong opposition to a creed. This is apparent in both groups and was supported by the example of American Congregationalism. We discussed this matter at length in the book, *This We Believe* and will not go into the details again.

Having recognized the obstacles the next question is, "What shall our fathers do about them?" Shall they give up and remain as isolated outposts carrying out only that part of the Great Commission which was within the local "scope and ability" or search for a way to greater things? In this they would need leaders. God, who promises to supply the needs and who gives gifts to the individual believers as well as gifts to the church, was ready to answer the prayers of the burdened ones for wisdom and for people to do the leading. This is the story in the next chapter.

FOOTNOTES—CHAPTER III

1. Except for two of the congregations, all still worship in the same locations. The Tabernacle is part of the Evangelical Mission Covenant. The Temple is, as already noted, the home of the Central Free congregation affiliated with the Evangelical Free Church of America. First Evangelical Free Church moved 47 blocks farther south in 1951. The Swedish Methodist Church was later known as Immanuel and a congregation of the United Methodist Church. It moved to a new building 12 blocks farther south and has recently merged with the Edgewater Methodist Church. The original building was destroyed by fire. Between that time and the completion of the new, the congregation met in the Swedish Temple.
2. Fredrik Franson, a few years later, met in a number of communities with congregations tracing their origin back to the Lammers Revival. Ingulf Diesen, head of the sister denomination in Norway, has written an excellent manuscript of the history of the Norwegian Mission Covenant in which he documents the connection between the Lammers revival; the one lead by Franson and the organizing of the Free Church in Norway in 1884.
3. The mistreatment of George Scott in Sweden, like that of Hauge in Norway, fanned the flames of rebellion.
4. The author is indebted to a biography of Paul Peter Waldenstrom, written in Swedish by N. P. Ollen, second edition published by the Swedish Mission Publishing House in 1917, for a most informative review of the role played by Waldenstrom in all three of the controversies.
5. The name Ansgar has special significance for those who know the history of Christianity in Scandinavia. Bishop and later Archbishop Ansgar (801-865) is recognized as the Apostle to the North. A Benedictine monk, he first went to Denmark and also worked in Sweden. Although the Scandinavian countries did not really turn to Christianity (Roman Catholic) until one hundred and fifty years later, he is looked up to as the first missionary to those countries. The name "Mission" Church or Synod is also significant as it implies the spirit of evangelism, the passion to share Christ, first with the people in the community, then across the nation and across the sea. All of the denominations have been known for their emphasis on missions.
6. *Sunshine and Shadows*, p. 144.
7. Schaff, Philip, *The History of Creeds*, Harper, NY, 1877, p. 826.
8. Walker, Williston, *Creeds and Platforms of Congregationalism*, Pilgrim Press, Boston, 1883, p. 441.

Chapter IV

THERE WERE GIANTS
IN THE EARTH

On one of many frequent visits to Oslo I attended the Bethlehem Church, the largest sister congregation in Norway. One of the leading "Bible women" was speaking. Her introductory story told of taking some children to a museum in which were displayed the extremes of nature's creatures from dinosaurs to germs so small they could be seen only with the aid of a microscope. One lad asked the guide, "How come there are no giant creatures today while we still have flies and mosquitos?" "I really don't know," was her reply, "except that the giants seem to have disappeared. Apparently they were destroyed in the ice age."

"There's an idea for a sermon," I thought, and proceeded to prepare one appropriate for anniversaries entitled "The Vanishing Giants" using as a text the statement, "There were giants in the earth in those days."[1] However, as one delves deeper and deeper into history he finds that while there were giants—spiritual as well as intellectual—in the beginning days of the Free Church movement, they are not necessarily a vanishing breed. It takes a generation of time to fully measure the stature of a leader. The founders were not always looked upon as giants by their contemporaries. They were often controversial, considered stubborn, impatient over delays, intolerant of contrary opinions. Some had visions those of shorter stature could not see. Only time and an examination of the fruits leads to the conclusion that some of these lived before their time and because they were giants often walked misunderstood and alone. The honor and credit now given was not invariably attributed to them from the beginning.

From the standpoint of contributions to history, the writer has discovered that some of the leaders who made the greatest impression and exercised a most powerful influence on his own life are not always those whose names appear in the research material. Most of us should be thankful to serve our own generation by the grace of God. Only a few are destined to influence the generations which follow.

In studying the events, the decisions, the influences which gave impulse and direction to the movement, I have looked in vain for the names, the acts and the statements of some of those whom I may have known and revered in childhood and youth. This is not to imply that their life work was in vain but to call attention to the fact that not all are called to be giants. God has his way of choosing and preparing a person for a special task. There are giants, no doubt, in our church today but only time will enable historians to identify them.

A biblical illustration supports the conclusion that not everyone who is in the limelight at a moment in time will automatically occupy much space in history. The evaluation of contemporaries might not be that of future historians. It takes special preparation by the Head of the Church who sees the potential, gives direction and moves the mind and spirit. During the years the appointed one is not consciously preparing for a certain challenge. Leadership that is sought does not result in true leadership. History shows that in most cases leadership is thrust upon one but he or she discovers training and experience has

47

prepared him for the role. As one is suddenly burdened with the new responsibilities he can see the divine guidance in the past. This gives the assurance so necessary.

An example is that of Peter and Paul. During the public ministry of Jesus, Peter was a leader. He was the first to speak, the first to act and also the first to fail. He was the first to confess that Jesus was the Christ, the Son of the Living God, a confession on which the Christian Church would be built. But some of these very personality traits might lead one to question his qualifications as the one who would interpret and introduce the great teachings of Christianity to the world. He was a lowly fisherman, impulsive, impatient, given to violence, but nevertheless a graduate of the three-year course in the school of Jesus, including the teaching and the field trips. He was an eyewitness to His life and work. He was the spokesman for the others. Was he not destined to become the one to introduce the plans for the church? During that very time God was preparing another man, a man who would have scoffed angrily at the suggestion that he was being prepared to lead the followers of Jesus and to become the instrument through whom the church would be established theologically and the message of God spread beyond the narrow confines of Judaism. Paul, who considered himself the last and least of the apostles, was prepared by training, temperament, conversion and a post-graduate course for the task. Israel's first Prime Minister, Ben-Gurion, said in my hearing that he had no quarrel with Jesus for he followed in the teachings of Judaism but "that man Paul" was the one he would like to have confronted for he was really the founder of Christianity. While one might challenge the conclusion, it was Paul who articulated and interpreted Christianity under the guidance, of course, of the Holy Spirit. It was also he who founded congregations in Asia and Europe.

The following will be a disappointment to some—the omission of names. We are restricting the list to those who played a leading role in the very beginning of the two Free Church movements.[2] There are many who appear upon the scene later without whose leadership the building on the foundation would not have been realized. But it was the earliest leaders who not only laid the foundation but, in a most remarkable twenty-five year period, trained those who followed.

It should also be noted that we are not reviewing the work of the pioneer evangelists, preachers and missionaries but those who actually participated effectively in laying the foundation not necessarily of the outreach but the organization. Nor were these the only giants but were key men at a critical moment who were able to persuade others.

The book marking the Golden Jubilee of the Swedish group pays a beautiful tribute to the giants which bears repeating:[3]

> In the history of every denomination there seems to be some outstanding person or persons in and around whom the work centers. This is especially true of the work as it was in the beginning. The life and work of certain individuals have woven themselves into the very fabric of the various denominations—persons who not only represented the work in question, but who were to a great extent the work itself. No matter how old a denomination may become or how widely it may have deviated from its original program, these persons will always keep their places and for all time exert a great influence.
>
> The Free Church is no exception to this. The pioneer leaders, though not many, were in their way and day great men. When one realizes the difficulties under which they had to labor, one appreciates the integrity and influence of these men and women of God.

In view of the events in the 1940s when the Swedish and Norwegian-Danish Evangelical Free Churches were moving towards the 1950 merger it is interesting (or should we say, it was providential) that each had leaders of similar qualifications in education and spiritual insight plus holding positions destined to mold the leaders of the next generation.

The one denomination was much younger than the other. The year the Swedes were meeting in Boone (1884), the first two congregations which would eventually become part of the Norwegian-Danish Evangelical Free Church Association came into existence. The first was organized at Tacoma, Washington, in January and called the Scandinavian Congregational Church; the second in Boston, Massachusetts, where the group started the same year but was not formally organized until 1885 and also called the Scandinavian Congregational Church.

Though the younger of the two, Boston is always looked upon as the "mother church" because of the subsequent development from there to the rest of New England and on to Chicago and Minneapolis, the centers of Norwegian-Danish populations. The Tacoma congregation (Elim) was somewhat isolated until the West Coast Missionary Society came into existence in 1910. It wasn't until 1907 that a second church in the area was organized. It might be said that Elim was the unmarried sister of the Boston church who married later in life and was renewed and had children!

It wasn't until 1886 that the third congregation came into existence at Wesley, Iowa, and interestingly was also called the Scandinavian Congregational Church. While there is a difference as to the time of beginning, the problems faced in forming a denomination were almost identical with those of the Swedish Free Church.

The leaders of both were men with an ecumenical rather than parochial vision. For example, the Swedish had its Princell while the Norwegians its Jernberg; the former its August L. Anderson and the latter its O. C. Grauer. Both had Fredrick Franson.

John Gustaf Princell was without question the foremost character in the Free (Swedish) Church movement, and in a sense its founder. To him it was given to be the leader preeminent for a considerable number of years. He was a

50

great man, head and shoulders above the others. He had a great mind that was motivated by a tender heart. He was a teacher of rare ability, especially for the student with sufficient capacity to assimilate the deeper and nobler things. He was a lover of big things and big people. He loved little people too, if they showed signs of growth or willingness to grow. He was a man of profound learning and had a wide range of gifts. This, together with his wit and humor made him very popular as a speaker.

A summary of his training and the controversies in which he was the center reveal the influences leading to what became an obsession—the independence of the local church. Though we cannot find he had any direct connection with American Congregationalism his statements, some of which are recorded elsewhere in this volume, indicate his image of the local church and inter-church relations were that of ultra-congregationalism.

Princell studied at the University of Chicago majoring in Latin, Greek and mathematics; and from there went on to additional training at the German American College in Philadelphia. Ordained in 1871 by the Augustana Lutheran Synod, his last official charge was pastor of the Gustavus Adolphus Church in Manhattan. He served as President of Ansgar College, 1880-84, and as associate editor of *Chicago-Bladet* beginning in 1884. He was head of the Free Church School from its earliest days until 1915.

He was forced out of the church in New York over serving communion to believers only and dismissed from the Lutheran Church Ministerial after a trial in 1878 because of his views on the doctrine of the atonement.

His experience at Ansgar College and Seminary in Knoxville, Illinois, was equally traumatic. Here he was accused of trying to sever the connection between the school and the Ansgar Lutheran Synod in order to make the former an independent and non-sectarian institution.

As a writer for the *Chicago-Bladet* he fought the concept of denominationalism in favor of local, independent congregations working together in association with each other, but not under the control of a national body. He contended for the congregational concept in which the national membership would consist of ministers and delegates not of member congregations. This led to the formation of two national bodies—the Swedish Covenant Church and the Swedish Free Church.

One tribute to his skill is interesting since it comes from one who would not have supported him. David Nyvall, the first President of North Park College, in his history of the Swedish Covenanters writing about Princell's role in the controversy leading to the development of the two denominations, deplored the refusal of the Covenant to allow Princell to speak at the organizing conference of the Covenant and mentions the resolution of apology adopted at the 1898 conference at Omaha in Princell's presence. Karl Olsson, in a footnote, observes:

> Nyvall's opinion in this matter is an excellent example of his largemindedness. It remains a question if organizations, even religious organizations, can exercise the same tolerance which we find so admirable in individuals. Princell posed a real threat to the organization of the Covenant, not because he was right, in which he should have been listened to, but because he was persuasive. The Covenant could not in this precarious situation permit itself the luxury of Princell's participation.[4]

Reinert A. Jernberg of the Norwegian group was a different type altogether. Since he was not as controversial, not as much has been written about him by early historians. Born in Norway, he, as many of his Norwegian contemporaries, went to sea. He was converted at the Seamen's Mission in Providence, Rhode Island, and settled in America in 1874. Upon completing preparatory training at Greenwich Academy, he went to Yale University graduating in 1884. After one year at Yale Seminary he transferred to the Chicago Theological Seminary, the Congregational school, where the additional two years of seminary education was completed. The second year at the school he was made an instructor in the Norwegian-Danish Department and in 1890 was made head of the department and held that position until it was discontinued following the establishment of the Free Church School at Rushford, Minnesota (later, moved to Minneapolis). He continued, however, to teach at the school until 1923. Jernberg moved west and served on the faculty of the University of Southern California, first as a teacher of Greek and later as librarian for the School of Religion. He kept up his contacts with the Free Church until his death in 1942. He was still department head in 1915 when the *Evangeli Budskab* was published.

Like Princell who promoted his views through *Chicago-Bladet,* Jernberg's influence in matters pertaining to church structure was widened through his editorship of the *Evangelisten*—the official paper of the Norwegian-Danish Free Church beginning in 1889. In 1902, through the new periodical, he became the first to promote the idea of a youth society in each local church. Following the organizing of the Western District, when churches in the Eastern areas did not respond to the invitation to a meeting to consider a national association, Jernberg went East and organized the Eastern District Association. There is this act and a number of other indications that Jernberg was more than a man who confined himself to the ivory tower. Like Princell, he was also active in the front lines! In addition to serving a number of Congregational Churches prior to joining the Seminary faculty, he held several positions in the Norwegian-Danish Association as well as editing the *Evangelisten.* Another evidence of his strong leaning toward congregationalism was the conflict with P. C. Trandberg, a Lutheran and head of the department in the Seminary, over Jernberg's acceptance of congregationalism and not Lutheranism.

A number of Trandberg's former students left the movement upon his resignation, in repudiation of Jernberg's views on church structure branding other Free Church leaders who followed Jernberg as heretics.

How great was the influence of these two giants? It would be difficult to overestimate when one considers the following:

In 1915 The Norwegian-Danish Association published a book of sermons by Free Church pastors including a brief biography of each. Of the 55 listed, 29 studied under Jernberg, 15 had no formal training, 7 had studied elsewhere and 4 at the new Free Church school, the first to graduate from it. Eight of those in the group with no formal training or from other schools were working in Norway and never did hold leadership roles in America. This means that of the 45 who did, 28 had been students under Jernberg.[5]

It has been estimated that as many as fifty to one hundred evangelists, pastors, and teachers working in the United States and Norway were trained under the leadership of Jernberg. As further evidence it is important to note that members on the original committee to plan for the establishment of the Free Church School (Bible Institute and Academy) were graduates of the Chicago Theological Seminary. Included were Jernberg and O. C. Grauer as well as L. J. Pedersen who became the Institute's first president. He was eventually joined on the faculty by C. B. Bjuge who was not only a graduate of the Chicago school but Carleton College as well, another congregational school, located in Minnesota. The faculty also included E. M. Paulson and two women (there was apparently no objection to having women teach future pastors!), Grace Skow (Mrs. E. M. Paulson) and Clara Reishus. The Swedish Schools had on its faculty Mrs. Josephine Princell and Miss Anna Lindgren who also taught the future leaders. Lindgren was a graduate of a seminary in Sweden.

Princell's influence runs a fascinating parallel. The Ministerial of the Swedish group published a book in 1945 similar to that of the Norwegian-Danish Association.[7] The Free Church School traces its orgin back very near to the beginning of the movement if one is to consider the special

54

Bible courses as part of the training program. Princell, though not the head of these, was on the committee. Eliminating all of those who were ordained after 1915 so as to compare with the other book we find that of the 46, 29 studied under Princell, 9 had no formal education and 8 had studied at other schools.[6]

This writer, though never having met Princell or Jernberg, has been told that he was brought as a child under five years of age to at least one meeting at which each had spoken. He was either too young to remember or slept through the scholarly hour to an hour-and-a-half sermon. I do not know if or when the two might have met each other, but it is reasonable to assume that they did. I have had many opportunities to talk to men who studied under them or to their sons and daughters. It has been apparent that the influence of these two over their students went far beyond the classroom lectures. Further, both instilled in their students what became a passion for the independence of a local church and the protection of the equality within the local membership. In other words, they sowed the seed of congregationalism.

There is also a contrast between the two men. Princell had suffered much at the hands of the Lutheran church. He has been called a wounded man. However, he did not attack the church directly but rather reacted through his ceaseless opposition to the very idea of Synods. "Synode er synd nog" (Synod is sin enough) was one of his battle cries. He opposed any attempt to organize the local congregations into a denomination as he interpreted that word. So strong was his personality and arguments that the position of the Free Church today reflects some of those views, though the denomination did not follow his theology in other matters.

Jernberg's experiences were quite different. He had apparently been turned off by the State Church in his youth. As we have noted, he was converted at a seamen's mission in America. All of his education which followed was in the schools of a denomination, the American Congregational, and it was along those lines that he drafted a blueprint for the Norwegian-Danish Association of Churches. He would have disagreed with Princell in the latter's opposition to denominationalism as perceived by him. Nevertheless, it comes as somewhat of a surprise to read his attacks on Lutheranism. These cannot be considered subjective as they would had they been spoken by Princell. Rather, they were objective. We are fortunate in having access to the speech Jernberg gave on the occasion of his installation as dean of the department at the seminary (1895). In speaking of the exodus from the church he first gives the reasons for the departure and then the two routes which the opposition took.

> The only church which until recently has had the molding and determining influence on the Scandinavian people is the Lutheran. For three hundred fifty years or more she has held undisputed sway over their spiritual and intellectual life. The result fills one with sadness. In England and America men have generally come to believe the Church of Christ the most potent power for the help and uplift of every man who comes under its influence. In Scandinavia they have come to think that before a man can be lifted out of his narrow, selfish, and often stupid views of life, he must come out from the Church, for it is her influence that is crushing all higher life out of her people. This explains the exodus from the church, on the one hand, of the men who are the intellectual leaders of the North today, the writers of its literature, who go on to infidelity; on the other hand of those who still believe in Christ, but failing to find it in the forms and ceremonies of a lifeless church, come out from it, and are like sheep having no shepherd, though looking for the true fold of Christ.

As to the first class, he concludes that they have left Christianity altogether although the influence of early teachers is evident in their support of social actions. As to the second group, he continues:

> Those who for conscience sake have separated themselves, the dissenters, have naturally no sympathy with this intellectual movement. They look with distrust upon an education with Christ left out of it. While, therefore, they have broken

with the Church because of her lack of life, they are no less suspicious of schools, for learning to them means only the hindrance and death of spiritual life. They do not want their leaders to be taught by men, but only by the Holy Spirit. All other learning is vain and puffed up. The prejudice against an educated ministry is greatly hindering the growth of the Free Church work in Denmark and Norway, and among their nationalities here. In Sweden, however, this feeling is rapidly disappearing before the influence of educated leaders and excellent free church seminaries.

It has seemed necessary to point out these two very opposite results of the rule of the Lutheran Church in Scandinavia in order to understand how much she may be relied upon as a factor in the development of Scandinavians in this country, for as she is there, so she is here, only modified by the irresistible influence of her environment.

The bone of the spiritual power of the Lutheran Church is this: She exists for herself and not for her people; she is not a means to an end, but is herself the end. She bears testimony to this in her attitude of opposition to every effort made by other Christian churches to elevate and convert the Scandinavian people. One of her ministers writing some years ago, and deploring the condition of his Norwegian countrymen here in Chicago, said, that of the 40,000 of them in the city then, all baptized and by law made members of the Church, not more than 5,000 of them could be found in her places of worship. Yet he branded every attempt by Christians of other denominations to draw some of the remaining 35,000 away from the saloons, beer gardens, and Sunday picnics, where he said a large number of them were to be found, as base and un-Christian efforts to proselyte, and steal them away from their spiritual mother. This is the spirit of the whole Church. In the first meeting of her united factions in America in 1890, the Norwegian United Church passed some resolutions especially aimed at our Congregational work, condemning and vigorously protesting all missionary efforts of other denominations among Scandinavians.

Lutheran preachers never miss an opportunity to tell us that the education and spiritual training of the foreigners is their business and not ours. But, in view of the results of that training in their old home, it seems a quite fair question to ask if we want them to continue that work here.

Jernberg then refers to the book by M. W. Montgomery, to be mentioned in more detail in a later chapter, which exposed some of the tragedies of the religious life in Scandinavia and caused a great commotion in the State Churches and their counterparts in America. He continues:

> When the light shines in upon a darkness that has not been broken for three hundred years it wakes to activity many drowsy creatures who vociferously protest against the intrusion. The development of the Scandinavians in this country to the ideas of our American life have been in spite of the influence of their mother church, not because of its help. Serious as this charge may be, it is amply proven by words and works of their teachers and preachers.
>
> In view of these facts, what is to be the attitude of the American Christians towards these people? Must we ask permission from the Lutheran Church who claims to own them, before we try to save those who are yet in their sins? Shall they perish because they find not the way to God through the portals of this particular church? Need we fear the charge of proselyting, where we labor simply to win men from the kingdom of darkness to the kingdom of light? Our Master's command was: "Go teach all nations," and lest we forget to go, he graciously brings the opportunity right to our doors. Again it seems as if the great shepherd of the sheep had especially committed to our care, that large number of earnest Scandinavian Christians who for conscience sake have separated themselves from the Church of their fathers, and who have no other affiliation. They stand nearest to us in their conceptions of faith and church policy. They themselves have recognized this kinship of spirit by repeated expressions of confidence in us.

Two giants—Princell and Jernberg. How interesting it would have been if providence had placed them in the same group but it may not have been for the best of the two groups, their beginnings and eventual merger. I am reminded of the answer given by one to the question, "Who would you rather have had for a wife, Martha or Mary?" "I'd like to have had Martha before dinner and Mary after dinner," was the reply. In answer to the hypothetical question, "Who would you rather have seen as the leader in the 1880s had the Norwegians, Danes and Swedes been together?" I would have answered, "I would like to have had Princell up to 1884 and Jernberg afterward!"

As the writer has studied these two giants from a long distance in time never having met them in person, there is nevertheless an image developed. Whether the image is right could be challenged by someone still living who was an adult in the last twenty years of the last century and has a sharp enough focus and whose memory may be trusted. The image includes the picture of two great men who had much in common. Both were born in Scandinavia but educated in the United States at prestigious schools. Both were scholars. Both were men of serious mien yet men of wit. Both had the gift of leadership and administration although Jernberg seems to have adapted himself more readily to the latter than Princell. Both were impatient. It has already been noted that Princell had little time to waste on those who were too lazy or lacked the ability to go with him into the deeper things of knowledge. Jernberg took organization matters into his own hands when things bogged down, as seen in the failure of the Eastern Congregations when they ignored the invitation from the Western Congregations to a meeting for the purpose of discussing organizing the two districts. Both men could be caustic. Jernberg's statement just quoted is ample evidence of that. An insight into Princell's use of sarcasm is revealed in his appraisal of the conference at Denver in 1905 as reported by Mrs. Josephine Princell in her biography of her husband:

> The conference business itself consisted of reports, discussions based on them, and decisions arising therefrom. Both morning and afternoon sessions began with a good time of prayer and short lecture on some topic that had been suggested—all in a reverent and worthy manner without any effort by those who took part to "make an impression." The evenings and Sunday were devoted exclusively to revival and devotional messages, preceded by a half hour of song, music and prayer . . . The sermons were pithy and fervent, for the

most part good, powerful and Spirit-inspired. There are always some strange and contradictory things that seem to take place at our Swedish Free Church meetings, even in the devotional sessions, as though the idea "free" had to be emphasized and illustrated in this way. One minister preached on "Hell" in both a serious and humorous manner, which showed that neither he nor the approving audience understood what was involved. Another spoke on "avoiding all appearance of evil." Something very sensible and solemn such as pointing out the sin of joking and poking fun might be presented in a joking and laughable manner.

Here are some of my impressions concerning the reports, discussions and similar proceedings. The reports from the officers, committees and branches of work were good enough, "in behalf of the work that was represented," but the contents were nothing of special interest. Much time, altogether too much, is spent at these meetings discussing trivial things, and this was no exception. Some of the speakers repeated themselves again and again as they took part in discussion. If they had something to say, I don't know, and maybe no one else knows, which reminds me of Lincoln's anecdote from the days when he helped operate the canal boats. Every time one of these steamboats which plied the Ohio River (back in the 1830's) blew its whistle—and that happened often—it ran out of steam; hence it made slow progress and could carry very little cargo. The application: Whistle less and pull more and get there faster! That is the impression I often get under the similar circumstances.

Above all else, both were men of God. Like Paul, they could not forget the day of their conversions. Both loved the Word of God, the Christian Church, and their students. We, in the Evangelical Free Church are richer because they chose to labor for and in our fellowship.

Not only was there a parallel in the leadership provided by Princell and Jernberg but the Swedish Free Church had August L. Anderson while the Norwegian-Danish had O. C. Grauer.

A. L. Anderson is called, in the Jubilee book, the man for the hour. For several years prior to his involvement in the founding of the denomination, he had been a member of an American Congregational Church and licensed as a lay preacher.[7] He was evidently a capable preacher even before completing his seminary training as evidenced by the report that he "was frequently called upon to preach during his student days." In 1877 he enrolled in the Ansgar College and before graduating was called to become pastor of a congregation in Colorado, a call which he accepted. After serving for one year he resigned to join the faculty at the Ansgar College. It's significant to note that this was when Princell took over the presidency. Among the many sources for controversy at the college was the clause in the constitution which held that the Augsburg Confession was the true expression of Biblical truth. This was supported by the Ansgar Synod which controlled the school. A. L. Anderson joined Princell in refusing to accept this position and with the support of another independent thinker, August Davis, they were leaders in preparing the way for the dissolution of the Synod in August of 1884 just six weeks before the meeting in Boone.[8] This also led to the closing of the school with the property going back to the city of Knoxville in Illinois.

A. L. Anderson, anticipating the closing, left the faculty after one year to become pastor of the Swedish Evangelical Free Church in Boone. As leader there he was destined to serve as host for the founding meeting in 1884 and play a leading role in the establishment of the denomination, a role for which his background and exceptional ability had prepared him. A study of the minutes of the conferences for the first two decades finds his name listed often as a member of standing and special committees, as well as moderator of conferences. He was called three times by the conference as General Superintendent of the newly formed "Free Mission" and served one term in that capacity. In 1885 he introduced and moderated the discussion on the subject, "*The Bible Basis for Order in the Congregation.*" Following his pastorate at Boone, he moved on to other pastorates completing his sixty-year ministry on the East

Coast serving other than Free Churches, since the latter had no congregations in that area, but retaining his affiliation with his first love.

This writer has the impression that A. L. Anderson was not only an outstanding pulpiteer, but an extraordinary administrator. The minutes always list the names of those participating in the discussions of the special subjects with the actual comments of each appearing eventually in *Chicago-Bladet.*

In the minutes of 28 meetings covering the first twenty years (they sometimes met twice during the year) he is mentioned only three times as particpating in the discussions. The one was at the first meeting in Boone when the delegates were forming the statement on the structure of the church and the second was in 1888 when he participated in the discussion of the question, "Does the Word of God permit a woman to appear as a preacher, take part in the general Christian work and have a voting right in the urgent matters before a congregation?" As on the other two occasions, the question had to do with the structure of the church. The third was in 1889, again at Boone, when the subject for discussion included the question, "What does the Word of God teach about the work of the congregation—edification and discipline, the services, spiritual gifts, teachers, salaries, and fund raising, etc.?"[9]

Princell and A. L. Anderson are from this distance a study in contrasts. The former, a great scholar, teacher, often bombastic, emotionally scarred by his experience at the hands of the Synod, obsessed with a passion for independence; but struggling with the question of the position of the local church in the framework of a larger fellowship. Anderson, on the other hand, was already committed to the form of independence found in the framework of Congregationalism. He brought an added dimension to the leadership. Whereas the others were recently out of the background of the Lutheran Synod, he had already spent several years in the American Congregational Church.

There are a few clues to his ability. The only occasion on which the introduction of the conference subject is stated with a complimentary adjective was when he spoke at the 1889 meeting. The recorder states that he gave a "moving" presentation of the question. The anniversary book published in 1914 refers to him as a "man richly endowed as a preacher and a solid, stable character."

Like the other pioneers he was, above everything else, an evangelist and soul winner. In a letter written in 1934 to the Golden Jubilee Conference from Wooster, Massachusetts, and published later in the *Beacon* (June 19) he wrote:

When I sit down and meditate on the past, there are innumerable incidents that pass in review which make me thankful to the Lord for saving me and calling me to be a messenger of the glorious gospel of Jesus Christ.

Not only occurrences but persons and places become so full of interest. The Rocky Mountains, for instance. There I went up and down among the hills and valleys seeking the lost. Often did I go to a mining camp for an evening or two, to tell the gruff miners of Him whose love would not let us go. And how glad I was when they would forsake their evening's sport and come to the meeting.

Among the brethren with whom I have been intimately connected in the evangelistic work was Frederick Franson. When I was in Colorado in 1878-79 he was in Utah trying to lead the Mormons into the light. Many years afterward, when he started to send out missionaries to China he had his first Bible course with us in Brooklyn, N.Y. He was very anxious to have me go and lead the first group that went out, but my large family made it impossible for me to go. The church in Brooklyn needed me also at that time. We had wonderful blessings from the Lord for a number of years.

For the benefit of the young people I wish to tell of an episode that took place during my second visit in Colorado. Leadville is one of the towns high up in the mountains. I went up there one Saturday to see if we could hold some meetings there. Looking around the town I found that there was no Swedish church but that there was a saloon that was known as "the Swedes' church." I hired the Y.M.C.A. meeting hall for Sunday afternoon. And after putting an advertisement in the evening paper I went up to the so-called "Swedish church." It is needless to say that I found what I was looking for. The place was filled with men who were handing their hard-earned money over the bar. I invited them all to the meeting next day, and praise the Lord, I got a goodly number of them. Among the crowd of men was a woman—a Christian woman.

When I came back to Denver and told of conditions in Leadville there were two young men who were so touched that they resolved to go there and preach the Gospel to the people. Their names were Herlin and Oscar Johnson. They had to support themselves, so they took turns—one working in the mines while the other made house-to-house visits, and then they held meetings in the evenings and on Sundays. People were saved and a church was built.

I have related this to encourage the young people of the Free Church to continue in the service of the King.

O. C. Grauer, a man known to the writer since early childhood and one of his heroes, was God's gift to the Norwegian-Danish Association. Born in Norway in 1859, he emigrated to America at the age of 4 and was converted in his youth at the Tabernacle (Congregational Church in Chicago) of which Dr. F. E. Emrich was the pastor. He and a Swede named Carl Bloomquist were the first and only students to enroll in the new Norwegian-Danish department of the Chicago Theological Seminary in September of 1884. He graduated in 1887. After serving American congregations for four years he returned to the Seminary as a member of the faculty along with Jernberg. In 1907 he was installed by the Congregational Home Mission Society as the superintendent for missionary work among the Danes and Norwegians. A year later he was also made superintendent for the work among the Slavics and the Poles. In 1921, following Risberg's death, the Swedish work was added.

During the years which followed he visited most if not all of the congregations then existing in the Norwegian-Danish Association and was a leader in its organization.

In 1889 Grauer, together with two others and with counsel from the Congregational Home Mission Society, planned the publication of a paper in Norwegian, the

Evangelisten. He compiled and translated into Norwegian a handbook for pastors in 1898 and a year later did the same with a Free Church catechism. In 1909 when the matter of uniting the Eastern and Western (the Middlewest) Associations both he and Jernberg, in true congregational tradition, opposed the suggestion that a creed would have to be drafted. Jernberg wrote:

> We have existed twenty-five years without a confession of faith, why should we have need of it now? We are attacked on every side, and putting our faith in writing will give our opponents a chance for definite charges. It is a step backwards. We have tried all these years to set people free from popery, and now we are going back into it ourselves.

The experience since 1909 proves that he was in error. Our light should not be hid under a cloak of secrecy.

Grauer took a similar position in the beginning. He said in a discussion in 1896, while still on the faculty at the seminary, "We need no confession of faith. The Association is practical and has no bearing on theology. It is to promote mutual fellowship and harmony among churches uniting them to do a common work." He was supported by the district superintendent of the American Congregationals, "Discussing creeds is a sign of spiritual decay." However, they really contradicted themselves when the superintendent suggested that the delegates and pastors go on record in approval of the Apostolic Confession and the Declaration of Faith as adopted by the National Congregational Commission in 1883. Grauer, however, after spending some time with the grass roots reversed his position and wrote, "A congregation according to the New Testament must have a confession of faith."

While the purpose of this volume is to present the search and finding of a pattern for church structure and not other doctrines or even an entire creed, we relate the above to add another link between American Congregationalism and the new Free Church movements.

In a tribute to Grauer in the March 11, 1931, issue of

Evangelisten on the occasion of his retirement from his work in the Congregational Home Mission Society, the name of Jernberg was also mentioned:

> We now have at least 66 congregations in the Association. Most of these were founded by the servants of our Lord who sat at the feet of these two well-known master-teachers. In addition to these there are capable leaders in other denominations who also studied at the same school. Neither the leaders nor the congregations with whom these made contact will forget the love and concern they had for our dear Norwegian-Danish people.

The tribute stated that there were no more outstanding theologians among the Norwegians in America during that period than these two. They were original, practical and left eternal blessings.

It could be said that Jernberg was the Paul, Grauer the Barnabas, C. T. Dyrness the John Mark, L. J. Pedersen, the Apollos of those beginning years. Evidence of the great appreciation of Grauer by the American Congregational Home Missionary Society is shown in that he was honored on his retirement at the church in Brooklyn, N.Y., made famous by the ministry of Henry Ward Beecher, with the president of the National Conference of Congregational Churches as speaker.[12]

Fredrik Franson belonged to both Free Church movements and was another influence in the formative years. Contrary to the general impression that Franson was primarily and even only a missionary to overseas fields, he was an outstanding churchman long before he sensed a call to fields abroad. He had already worked in America and Scandinavia before conducting the services in Germany where he first heard the call for missionaries to China.[11]

Born in Sweden in 1852, he studied in a preparatory school at Nora and enrolled later at the college of Orebro (a secondary school). He moved with his parents to America in 1869 settling in Nebraska. He was converted during a long illness in 1871-72 and proved to be one of those special servants, unschooled and yet bestowed with many gifts including remarkable insight. His first book was on the structure of the congregation according to the New Testament. Sensing the need for trained workers, he started holding special Bible courses, first for men and women who would become evangelists in America. It was only later that he turned to the training of missionary candidates. He led the way for equal opportunities for both men and women to be witnesses and wrote a pamphlet, "The Prophesying Daughters" to provide a Biblical support for the conviction that the Great Commission was not for men only. His experience in administrative affairs contributed much to the churches which were born in the revivals among Scandinavians. For example, at the early age of 22 he served as regional secretary to the Baptist Council which gave official recognition to the Swedish Baptist Church. In 1896 at a meeting of the Swedish Free Church at Joliet, Illinois, he presented a plan to unite the three Swedish "Free" groups; namely the Evangelical Free, the Mission Covenant (Evangelical Covenant), and the Scandinavian Congregational Churches.

In 1975, Missionary Edvard Torjesen, speaking at the 95th anniversary of the congregation in Westmark, Nebraska, revealed the many contributions of this man to the founding of churches in that state.[12] These were to become part of the nucleus of the group to eventually meet in Boone in 1884. The congregations at Phelps Center (Monroe), Westmark, Keene, and Industry were all started within a ten-day period and Fredrik Franson was at all four constitutional meetings! As the conflict between the Mission and Ansgar Synods intensified, he wrote an article on church organization published in *Chicago-Bladet* in May of 1879 in which he suggested:

1. That each congregation act as its own synod;
2. That each congregation develop its leadership from among its own members on the pattern of prophets and teachers,

elders, and deacons, and evangelists in the New Testament local churches;

3. That each congregation should express its solidarity with other congregations . . . also on the pattern of the New Testament local churches . . . through the ministry of itinerant evangelists and missionaries, both its own as well as those of local congregations.

Franson was in Europe during the years when the Swedish Free and Covenant were organized as two separate bodies but his influence leading up to 1884 and later cannot be overlooked.

These then are some of those who provided the initial leadership in the search for identity.

There are a few additional items of interest in connection with the congregational influence. The second meeting of the Swedish Free Church group was held in Minneapolis in a Congregational Church.

The first missionary to be sent to China, following the decision of the 1885 conference was H. J. Von Qualen, a graduate of Chicago Theological Seminary. He began his ministry, even before going to China, by teaching a class of Chinese men in one of the Congregational churches in Chicago. Two of the men won to Christ, Eugen Sieux and John Lee, joined him in the work in China. On the occasion of his commissioning in 1887 representatives of the seminary and the American Congregational Church took part as well as Princell and another Free Church leader, J. W. Stromberg.

Yes, there were giants in the earth in those days! But without followers there could have been no leaders!

The next chapter will discuss the patterns for church structure as had recently been adopted by the Congregationalists—patterns of which these knowledgeable leaders and many others were aware since they were currently topics of discussion in the press and religious periodicals at the very time our founders and their followers were searching for identity.

Footnotes—Chapter IV

1. Genesis 6:4
2. The Swedish Evangelical Free Church and the Norwegian-Danish Evangelical Free Church Association merged in 1950. Both sought and found similar identities.
3. The Golden Jubilee of the Swedish Evangelical Free Church was compiled by E. A. Halleen, William B. Hallman, Milton G. Nelson, G. A. Young and published in 1934. The tribute appears on p. 14.
4. Nyvall, David, *The Swedish Covenanters*, 1954 Covenant Press, Chicago, Ill., p. 61, Footnote. In spite of the differences which led to the formation of the two Swedish denominations David Nyvall and J. G. Princell were close friends until the latter's death in 1915 for it was Nyvall who was asked by the Princell family to speak at his burial. Nyvall said in part:

   He was as original as he was eloquent. He studied other minds, he spoke his own mind, his own heart. He was in all things independent, and would rather solve a problem himself even at the risk of a faulty solution, than let others solve it for him.

   He was a genius, he was not only original in most things, but in many things an originator. He often said things strikingly new, and more often said old things in a strikingly new manner. In this, I believe, lay his greatest gift as a lecturer, always interesting, always abundantly entertaining, never tiresome.

   We stand in a debt of gratitude to him as to no other teacher, a debt which, I am sorry to say, has not been paid and most probably shall never be paid, and yet a debt which should at least be acknowledged. He taught many who are now teachers and leaders.

5. Some of the outstanding preachers and leaders in both groups had no formal education. This is not to support the idea that only the Holy Spirit and not schools should prepare men and women for the ministry. In my student days, I was told that I had to make a choice between education and fervency of spirit. I would also run the risk of having the Lord return while I was still in school thus robbing me of the opportunity to engage in the urgent task of soul-winning. Among those who had no formal education was N. W. Nelson, probably the outstanding pulpiteer in the Norwegian Church, and E. A. Halleen, the similarly gifted preacher in the Swedish Church who served as its president for so many years. The book referred to was *Evangeli Budskab*: sermons and biographies compiled by C. B. Bjuge, C. T. Dyrness, K. P. Wuffestad, and E. N. Reiersen and published by the Evangelisten Publishing Society in 1915.
6. *Laborers Together With God*: compiled by John E. Dahlin, Frank W. Anderson, and Philip C. Hanson and published by the Ministerial Association of the Evangelical Free Church (Swedish) in 1945. These two volumes by the two groups are invaluable in providing information about the men as well as their thinking.
7. Golden Jubilee, op. cit., p. 18.
8. August Davis was the first pastor of the First Evangelical Free Church in Minneapolis, 1885-1896.
9. The subjects to be discussed were published in advance. A. L. Anderson's statement appeared later in *Chicago-Bladet*: "I will read some verses from Luke 8. Then we shall see what women may do in Jesus fellowship. It says they followed him and served him with their substance. Among these were both single and married women. What do we do more than serve him? May

the spirit of muteness flee from both men and women for it is dreadful how silent we have become about the Lord and his grace both in our homes and at social gatherings as well as in the circle of the fellowship. Where two or three are gathered in His name, that is the fellowship of believers." The women discreetly stayed away from the 1888 meeting but it was reported, according to the minutes that Ellen Modin had gone to Utah (to evangelize among the Mormons) accompanied by Lottie Anderson and that they would soon be assisted by another woman, Mathilda Johnson. It was also reported that nurse Elizabeth Nyrop was going to China. Further, Mrs. Josephine Princell whose name often appeared among those who participated in conference debates, also avoided the meeting and sent the report of her activities by letter. It would seem that some wanted to close the door to service after the servants had gone forth, sent by and supported financially by the Free Church. Of the 12 who were quoted only 3 were opposed. Anderson's support with his congregational background coincides with the support given Ellen Modine by R. A. Jernberg who was then head of the Norwegian-Danish Department of the Chicago Theological Seminary.

10. *Evangelisten,* March 11, 1931, in an article by Pastor Ole Thompson.

11. It was while in Germany, after having been released from prison in Denmark and banished for life, that he read of J. Hudson Taylor's plea for 1,000 missionaries for China. He began where he was and appealed for 50 volunteers from Germany. The Evangelical Alliance Mission was formed which is today the overseas arm for the Free Evangelical Churches of Germany.

12. Edv. J. Torjesen has prepared an excellent manuscript on Frederik Franson as a churchman.

70

Chapter V

THERE WAS ALSO THE GENEROUS UNCLE

𝕴t should be apparent by now that the American Congregationalists played an important role in the earliest years of the history of The Evangelical Free Church of America. The *direct* influence was greater on the Norwegian-Danish Evangelical Free Church Association than on the Swedish Evangelical Free Church. This is not to conclude that the influence on the Swedish community as a whole was any less. If general influence could be measured, it was greater. It is also apparent that this was not appreciated as greatly by the Swedish groups during the 1880s as by the others.

Karl Olsson, the historian of the Evangelical Covenant Church, with not a little sarcasm, in summarizing why the Swedish Mission Friends were attracted to the Congregationalists—the "ecclesiastical, organizational and spiritual affinities,"—claims that the strongest hold of the American church upon the immigrants was economic. "Like a fairy godmother, the Congregational Church stood ready to change the pumpkins of indigence into chariots of relative security in a new world."[1] This analysis would not necessarily reflect the opinion of all of the leaders in the 1880s.

I was brought up under the influence of the men who studied at the Congregational Seminary. Because of the hospitality of my parents, I met, in our home, most of the pastors and other leaders in the 1910-1930 decades.[2] L. J. Pedersen, a graduate in 1899, organized congregations even before entering the school and was later president of the new Norwegian-Danish school from 1910-1932. He was also a co-founder of the congregation in Minneapolis of which my parents were charter members. I was confirmed by Pedersen and received both my academy and seminary diplomas from him. I studied theology under C. B. Bjuge and was taken by C. T. Dyrness, a superb organizer and successful pastor, under his wings as a young pastor. These men were dedicated to the cause of the Norwegian-Danish work. Not once in my close association with these elders and others did I sense anything but gratitude to the "generous uncle."

Before going into the specifics of the contributions of the Congregational Church it would be well to consider, briefly, the history of that church and remind the reader that the Congregational Church we are considering as aiding in the search for identity is the church as it was in the 1880s and 1890s and not what it was before or what it has become since.

The founders in the latter half of the 19th century would have felt comfortable with the views of the pilgrims on the complete separation of the church from the control of civil authorities. After all, they had gone through experiences in Scandinavia at the hands of the Lutheran-State combine similar to those of the separatists at the hands of the Anglican-State combination in England. But that rapport would soon have given way to a separation. While the pilgrims had enjoyed the experience of religious freedom in Holland, the freedom in the colonies became restrictive and available only to those belonging to the one church. The Puritans, coming a little later directly from England, "brought with them not merely a church; but a civilization . . . one which called for both a state and a church interlaced in such a way that the declarations of a town meeting or a general court often became the platforms for ecclesiastical procedure.[3] While there were the conferences of voluntary associations, the authority regarding the establishment and maintenance of the churches was with the state in Connecticut until 1818 and in Massachusetts until 1834. Note the dates as they are significant for the events in 1884. For the first two hundred years these colonies and later states performed as a denominational framework for the churches.

The founders of the Evangelical Free Churches would also have been comfortable with the early policy of a church membership restricted to believers only.

> The doors of the churches of Christ upon earth, do not by God's appointment stand so wide open, that all sorts of people, good or bad, may enter therein at their pleasure, but such as are admitted thereto as members, aught to be examined first, whether they be fit and meet to be received into the church society or not . . . the things which are requisite to be found in all church members, are repentance from sin, and faith in Jesus Christ; and therefore these are the things whereof men are to be examined at their admission to the church, and which they then must profess and hold forth in such sort, as may satisfy rational charity that the things are there indeed.[4]

It wasn't long, however, before the churches were forced to compromise, a natural consequence of the policy of combining the church and the state. Only those who were members of the church could vote in the town meetings dealing with matters pertaining to civil as well as church affairs. The above-quoted test for membership was a natural for the first generation settlers. In the beginning the settlers insisted that the children of church members were also members on the basis of a covenant

73

patterned after the Old Testament covenant for the people of Israel. This inconsistency created a dilemma. How could the right to vote be given to those who, upon reaching adulthood, had not met the requirements for church membership? A compromise was agreed upon in some communities, after much and bitter debate, known as the Half-Way Covenant. This gave a standing in the church to those offspring who may have been moral but not regenerated. Thus was created a half-way house between the world and full Christian discipleship (1650-1660).

The founders of the Evangelical Free Churches would not have accepted the Half-Way Covenant nor the congregational system as compromised during the period of Presbyterian-Congregational cooperation. This has already been alluded to. There developed an interchange program, as civilization began to move west and beyond the borders of the New England colonies, between the Congregational Associations and the General Assembly of the Presbyterian Churches in America. The arrangement known as the Plan of Union was dropped in the middle of the last century. Three irreconcilable differences caused much debate and resulted in many accusations from both sides. The first was the difference in church structure, the second the authority of ministers, and third, the restrictions of an ultra-Calvinistic doctrinal position. All three would have created problems for the founders in the 1880s.

The nineteenth century saw a spiritual revival in America greatly affecting the Congregational Societies resulting in a slowing down of some of the consequences. Her "history had been one of strength and of weakness, of apprehensions of divine truth and of mistakes. The intermingling forces of the human and divine unfolding of the Kingdom of God on earth must ever be so. The fathers of the sixteenth and seventeenth centuries, applying the Reformation principles of the Authority of the Word of God to polity as well as to doctrine, sketched out the essential features of a Congregational Church as they believed it to be divinely appointed."[5] The return to the original principles was one which made those of 1880-1900 more compatible to the Free Church founders. The concept of a church-state relationship had been dropped long before. The Congregational principles of democracy within the church are even reflected in the Constitution of the United States.

A series of conferences resulted in declarations which brought the churches back to their earlier positions. First, there was the Burial Hill Declaration in 1865; second, the Constitution for a National Council and the Oberlin Declaration of 1871; finally, the adoption of the "Commission" Creed of 1883. It took two and a half centuries for the local churches, the state and district associations to get to the place where they were willing to form a national body. The Creed of 1883 was adopted at the very time the Swedes as well as the Norwegians and Danes were struggling with the same problem. They reached their conclusions in two and one half decades, thanks in part, to the experiences of the American Congregationalists.

Some important points made it easier for those coming out of the Chicago Theological Seminary to introduce the system, especially into the Norwegian-Danish Association.

The Oberlin Declaration removed the restrictions of an exclusively Calvinist theology which had developed. This is clear from a statement by one of the historians:

> Its statement of faith, adopted at Oberlin, is valuable as illustrating the catholicity of spirit, which accompanied this growth of denominational consciousness. In matters of doctrine, the constitution is more important for what it does not affirm than for what it declares.[6] Though nowhere expressly stated, the understanding of Oberlin at its adoption, and the interpretation since usually put upon it, is that it holds out the olive branch of denominational fellowship to brethren of Arminian sympathies, and is but a further illustration of that desire not to limit Congregational brotherhood to those who hold exclusively the system known as "Calvinism."[7]

The purpose for a national organization also has a ring

familiar to those who have read the purpose of the Evangelical Free Church national association:

The Congregational churches of the United States, by elders and messengers assembled, do now associate themselves in National Council:

To express and foster their substantial unity in doctrine, polity, and work; and

To consult upon the common interests of all the churches, their duties in the work of evangelization, the united development of their resources, and their relation to all parts of the Kingdom of Christ.

The statement in the creed of 1883 on the independence of the local church became the pattern for statements by both the Swedish and Norwegian-Danish founders.

We believe that the Church of Christ, invisible and spiritual, comprises all true believers, whose duty it is to associate themselves in churches, for the maintenance of worship, for the promotion of spiritual growth and fellowship, and for the conversion of men; that these churches, under the guidance of the Holy Scriptures and in fellowship with one another, may determine each for itself—their organization, statement of belief, and forms of worship, may appoint and set apart their own ministries, and should cooperate in the work which Christ has committed to them for the furtherance of the Gospel throughout the whole world.

The statement adopted at Boone, Iowa, in 1884 includes some striking similarities:

1. The Church of God on earth consists of the entire multitude of born-again and to Christ-baptized persons, wherever they as such may dwell.
4. Always remembering that the Church is one in Christ; that he is the head of the Church, and that the Holy Spirit is the infallible leader into all truth, and that the Word of God, especially the New Testament, is the constitution of the Church and its unforgettable rule, therefore it behooves each group of believers to stand fast in the liberty wherewith Christ has made us free; i.e., individuals as well as collectively, we have the right and obligation to remain independent of all forms of church authority, and to keep ourselves out of all obligations that might curtail such

privileges and perfect liberty. But the local churches should therefore the more cooperate among themselves by means of conferences and societies as well as with individuals in whom they have confidence.

The Norwegians and Danes endorsed the Congregational statement of 1883:

> We believe the Church of Jesus Christ, the spiritual and unseen, consists of all believers in Jesus Christ. It is their duty to organize into local churches in order to establish churches, to encourage Christian fellowship and growth in grace, and to work for the salvation of souls. These churches together, and each by itself shall determine their confession of faith, their organization, and their form of worship. They can call and ordain their own pastors. They ought to work together for the spreading of the Gospel over all the world.

The founders also shared with the Congregationalists a concern that pastors might exercise an unscriptural authority over the local congregation or the denomination. The statement of 1865 declares: "The ministry of the Gospel by members of the churches who have been duly called and set apart to that work implies in itself no power of government, and that ministers of the Gospel not elected to any office in any church are not a hierarchy, nor are they invested with any official power in or over the churches." This revealed a change from the general view expressed by the declarations of the seventeenth century. The system of the nineteenth century was the logical outcome of a democratic ideal. The pastor may be, at the very most, merely the moderator of the deliberations of the membership.

While there is a great emphasis on the freedom of the local church to establish its own creed, in each of the three aforementioned groups there was also freedom to accept a statement mutually agreed upon. And that is what happened as it represented the consensus of the actual faith as a uniform witness to those seeking fellowship and those transferring from one community to another.

While we seek to limit ourselves to the search for structural identity it might be well to note the basic reasons for the absence of a continued fellowship with the American Congregationalists. The shift towards theological liberalism, already in evidence at the turn of the last century, eventually led to the decisions to establish our own seminaries. Further, the union of the Evangelical and Reformed denomination with the General Council of Congregational Churches (the name was changed from National Council) to form the United Church of Christ in 1957 with a presbyterian form of church government was a source of disenchantment even to many American congregationalists. Two new congregational groups resulted—the National Association of Congregational Churches organized in 1955 to maintain the historic position on church structure and the Conservative Congregational Christian Conference (Four C's) in 1949 in disagreement with the liberal tendencies of the denomination.

Now we turn to the contributions made by this benevolent uncle to the Scandinavian settlers.

The first was in the field of education as already noted in the previous chapter.

The Chicago Theological Seminary established the Norwegian-Danish Department in 1884 headed for the first six years by Peter Christian Trandberg, a graduate of the University of Copenhagen and a revivalist in Denmark before emigrating to America. He was followed by Reinert A. Jernberg from 1891 until the department was phased out in 1916. Jernberg stayed on as a teacher in the Union Theological School, which was formed after the Seminary merged with Chicago University, to accommodate the immigrants who may not have been able to meet the new, more stringent entrance requirements following the merger. From 1884 to 1901, of the 99 students enrolled 30 became pastors in congregational or free churches in the U.S. or Norway, 27 in Lutheran congregations, 2 missionaries, 3 teachers, 2 doctors, 1 judge and 6 remained at the school.

The Norwegian-Danish Department was smaller than the Swedish. This was also true of the numbers involved in the congregations as contrasted with the much larger Synods, as well as the Covenant and Free Church work among the Swedes. Jernberg explained the reasons in 1901. He observes that in comparison with the work accomplished by the "successors to the Pilgrims" among the Swedes in America the work among the Norwegians and Danes may seem insignificant. There are, he notes, several reasons for this. There were at that time twice as many Swedes in America as Norwegians and Danes combined. In Sweden during the latter part of the 1800s there had been great spiritual revivals whereas in the other countries the revivals had been "less lively" and the results smaller. There was also the national character of the people to consider. They were cautious and conservative. So much so that as great an exodus from the old boundaries of faith under the State Church did not take place. "For these and other reasons the principles of congregationalism was slower in winning acceptance among the Norwegians and Danes in America. Yet, in spite of all of this, the labors which have been laid down produced rich fruits which fills our hearts with great joy."[8]

The Swedish Department was established in 1885. Karl Olsson writes of the circumstances. The constitutional conference of what was to become the Swedish Covenant Church was held in Chicago, February 19 to 25, 1885:

At the conclusion of Thursday's deliberations there came to the scene of the impending nativity the three Magi of the infant Covenant: the Congregationalists . . . In 1884 a Danish-Norwegian teacher had been appointed to the Chicago Theological Seminary. Now the Swedes were about to be given the same offer. The American churchmen who visited the lowly Swedish brethren that wintery day in 1885 were not wealthy or noble or even wise in any ultimate sense; they were, nevertheless, much different from the people whom they were addressing. They walked in the security of 250 years of American tradition. They were conscious of having behind them a not inconsiderable part of American wealth.[9]

This committee offered to set up a Swedish Department and bring from Sweden a teacher, chosen by the new Swedish church, at the Americans' expense. The offer was accepted and an emissary sent to consult with Paul Peter Waldenstrom who recommended Fridolf Risberg. He was a graduate of the University of Uppsala in 1871 and ordained as a pastor in the State Church. In 1882 he left the church to become a Free Mission pastor. Risberg came to Chicago to head the new department; and like Waldenstrom later, he apparently became enamoured with the Congregationalists as is reflected in the number of his Swedish students who joined them. From 1885 to 1905 of the 245 students enrolled, 150 became pastors in the Swedish-American congregations. In 1894 he officially joined the Congregationalists. This was not exactly what the Swedish Mission people had anticipated.[10]

The results created not a little opposition from the Swedish Covenant. By 1906 as Olsson reports: "There were 106 Swedish congregational churches. Some of these were built where Covenant congregations were already in existence. And at least in one district, Minnesota, the Swedish Congregational pastors had their own ministerial association apart from the Covenant."[11]

But one must not overlook the generosity of the Americans whatever their motives which this writer believes to be in the tradition of all who seek to carry out the great commission and are not bound by ethnic origin or language. Tuition at the Seminary was free, rooms were rented at one dollar a week, assistance was given in repaying funds borrowed in order to emigrate to America for study, and 12 scholarships were made available annually ranging from 40 to 75 dollars. A similar program was in effect for German and Welsh immigrants. The total cost to the departments for the first fifteen years was at least $120,000 with all but $2,000 coming from the Americans.

The second form of assistance was in the area of home missions. One of the concerns of the Congregational Churches in the earlier days was that of evangelism, a concern very much accelerated following the great American revivals in the 18th century. In the absence of a national organization, societies were formed to engage in home missions. A Home Mission Society was formed in Connecticut in 1798, the first such voluntary missionary society in America, which had as its purpose "to Christianize the heathen in North America and to support and promote Christian knowledge in the new settlements in the United States." The Massachusetts Missionary Society was founded in 1799 and the New Hampshire Society in 1801. An attempt was made (1826) to form an American Society to include the Congregational, Presbyterian, Dutch Reformed and the Associated Reformed. The latter three withdrew after a brief time to form their own denominational home missionary departments. When the National Association was formed (1893) the name of the society was changed to the Congregational Home Mission Society. Thousands of missionaries were sent to every state and territory in the union. In the 19th century alone, the Society organized or aided more than 5000 churches.[12] Among the beneficiaries of this Society were the Swedish, Norwegian and Danish immigrants—those who were no longer under the domination of the Lutheran State Churches in their former homelands or of their counterparts in America. The ministry to these ethnic groups in the languages of the countries from which they had come was at the right time and in the right place—one for which the descendants of the early immigrants should thank God upon every remembrance!

It would be difficult to provide an accurate figure of how many of the oldest congregations in what was the Norwegian-Danish Association received assistance because the statistics made no distinction between those who, as Scandinavian congregations, eventually became part of the American and those whose connections remained under the influence of the Scandinavian and became members of the Swedish Covenant, Swedish Free, and Norwegian-Danish Free. The Americans subsidized local pastors and provided both loans and grants to erect churches. As to money, it is estimated that at least $386,625 was provided for aid in training and supporting workers during just the first 15 years.

The generosity of the "Uncle" also made personnel available to the immigrant congregation—not only home missionaries, but extremely well-qualified superintendents supported by the Americans and assigned to assist these new groups of believers in every way possible. There were several whose contributions may well have been overlooked and whose names do not appear in the historical books of the Free Church.

There were three such superintendents. The earliest was Marcus Whitman Montgomery (1839-1894) who first comes to our attention as superintendent in Minnesota and North Dakota for the Congregational Home Mission Society with his headquarters in Minneapolis. It was while holding that position that he, through the generosity of an American jurist, E. S. Jones, a member of the Board of the Minnesota Home Mission Society, was able to visit the Scandinavian countries arriving in Stockholm on February 20, 1884. His interest in Scandinavia had been greatly aroused in a speech made by a Swedish pastor, George Wiberg [13]at the January meeting of the Congregational Club of Minnesota. Wiberg was a member of the Swedish Ansgar Synod! In the address he spoke of the progress being made in the home missionary work among the Swedes and said that these converts were not only evangelical mission friends but also "self-governing and independently in heart and soul congregationalists."

By 1880 there were 194,337 Swedes, 181,729 Norwegians, and 64,196 Danes in America. Montgomery was convinced that the American Home Mission Society could not properly ignore a people so intimately linked to the future growth of several states and all the territories. The

82

religious situation should be accurately known so as to determine if the Home Mission Society should help support the preaching of the Gospel among them. Before leaving for Scandinavia inquiries were made of the Society's missionaries in the field as well as workers under the American Sunday School Union concerning the habits and religious conditions among the Scandinavians in the United States. He declared that the information could be summarized as follows:

The information gathered may be summarized thus: *The Scandinavians are, all things considered, among the best foreigners who come to American shores.* For a republic where there is civil and religious liberty, and especially where these principles are the very corner-stone of the State, that foreign element is most desirable which most readily swings into the current of American life, and becomes inspired with the genius of American institutions. They who love liberty *and* religion will make the best citizens for this republic. Just such are the Scandinavians. They are almost universally Protestants; comparatively few of them are sceptics. They have been reared to believe in God, the Bible, the Sabbath, and in salvation through Christ. They ardently love the principles upon which our republic rests, and hence are intensely loyal. In politics they are generally Republican. They have large, strong bodies; are industrious, frugal, eager, apt, modest, intelligent. Very many American homes are blessed with the services of Scandinavian girls whose ways are likely to be honest, quiet, faithful, cleanly, and pious. Scandinavians are not exclusive nor clannish as to occupation or location. They are in every profession—are ministers, lawyers, physicians, teachers; are also in every business—farmers, manufacturers, merchants, bankers, artisans, miners, and day-laborers. They come here to stay; buy real estate, build good houses, found academies and colleges; and tens of thousands more from the "Land of the Midnight Sun" are following them hither . . .[14]

Their religion is not hostile to free institutions; they do not come here temporarily, and, while seeking for gain, live a foreign life, praying all the while that their bones may yet lie in the lands from which they came; they do not seek to break down (what there is left of) the American Sabbath; they do not make the United States the plotting-ground against the Government of their native land; they do not seek the shelter of the American flag merely to introduce and foster among us ideas in direct variance with all the most precious interests of our land—socialism, nihilism, communism; and they are not always intimating that the lands from which they came and their entire civilization are so much better than the country of their adoption. This republic—the hope and inspiration of the world—has nothing to fear from Scandinavians, but very much to gain. After a careful observation of these people in this land and in their native countries, I am clearly of the opinion that *they are more nearly like Americans than are any other foreign peoples.* In manners and customs, political and religious instincts, fertility of adaptation, personal appearance, and cosmopolitan character, they are strikingly like native Americans. No peculiar physiognomy is stamped upon them to point them out the world over; they find the English language easy, and quickly acquire it and lose their own brogue. The first generation of American-born Scandinavians, when they reach the age of twenty years, cannot generally be distinguished from Americans by either appearance, language, or customs.

In vices they are also much like Americans. Intemperance is sometimes said to be their national besetting sin. Like other Northern nations, they have a partiality for the stronger liquors as against wines and beer; and yet too many of them accept anything that will intoxicate. As regards profanity, gambling, and licentiousness, they are much in need of the converting power of the gospel.[15]

He carried with him a recommendation from his good friend, Skogsberg, pastor of the Swedish Tabernacle in Minneapolis, to the leaders of the Free Mission Societies in Sweden and a letter from the Minnesota Home Mission Societies as follows:

That our brother, the Rev. Marcus W. Montgomery, in his proposed trip to Sweden, be requested to bear Christian salutations of the congregational churches of Minnesota to the Mission Churches in that country, and to express our belief that in doctrine and polity we are substantially one; to greet them as our brethren in Christ; and to assure them of our hope that at no distant day formal and friendly relations will be established between us.

Enroute to Scandinavia, Montgomery stopped briefly at

the headquarters of the Congregational Churches in England where he was informed that, "Congregationalists in Sweden? No. There are only State Church Lutherans." One official told him that he had recently heard a rumor similar to that which had reached the brethren in the U.S. but whether the facts were as reported he could not say. The visitor from Minneapolis had been thoroughly misled by his brothers in London. In Scandinavia, people in general were reluctant to recognize the existence of the Mission Societies. For example, in Norway he secured a guide to help him locate the Mission Society meeting place in Oslo. He was told there was no such place. Nevertheless, he located Mr. M. M. Hansen, leader of the group who provided a new guide and interpreter after the first one had been fired. This was at the very time of the great Franson revivals and when the new Mission House was under construction in Oslo. The year was 1884 when the Swedish Mission Covenant was already six years old and the Norwegian Covenant about to be organized! How different he found things when he came to Scandinavia.

> I found that the Lord was again repeating in Sweden and Norway the historic providences by which three centuries ago, He led forth His people from the National Church of England to plan churches on the new Testament plan, both in England and the new world.[16]

Not speaking the Scandinavian languages (he learned them later) and finding few of the Covenant leaders who could interpret, he had some difficulty at the headquarters in Stockholm. But like a "dog who has picked up the scent, he searched for the evidences of congregationalism." To find Scandinavian congregationalists had become an obsession. Maundy Thursday was a great day in Sweden and made even more so by the visit of Waldenstrom to Stockholm where he spoke in a mission chapel to 1500 and again to 3000 the next morning. Montgomery, who by then had the benefit of an interpreter, was deeply moved. There was a remarkable power over the audience. The preacher stood and spoke fervently, with few gestures. There was no manuscript. The language was simple and the message filled with illustrations presented with astonishing clarity. A spirit of reverential silence prevailed over the audience. Was this, he thought, the Swedish congregational movement? If so, it was a good demonstration of spontaneous, evangelical congregationalism.

But he was to be more convinced later as he met with the head of the new Swedish Covenant Church and the rector of the school. He, and other members of the faculty, could understand English and some even speak it. There he could discuss church polity as it pertained to free and independent congregations and such matters as baptism and communion. He was also told of their membership being limited to believers while open to all believers. Montgomery left Sweden convinced that they were congregationalists as far as church structure and practices were concerned. The matter of what position the people had taken relative to Lutheran theology was not important to his interest at the time, which was mostly restricted to church polity.

From Stockholm he went to Oslo and made contact with some mission friends in that city. At that time plans were already underway for a constitutional convention scheduled for that summer. He writes of attending a service on a Day of Prayer. Here he heard a sermon preached by Severin K. Didriksen, "a Norwegian youth of about 22 years, fine looking, robust, earnest, humble, consecrated, who had then been engaged in evangelistic mission work for five and one-half years, even though he had enjoyed little training."[17]

This would be the right spot to inject an additional word about S. K. Didriksen. He emigrated to America that same year, (1884) founded the "mother church" of the Norwegian-Danish Association—The Norwegian Free Congregational Church of Boston—went on to graduate from the Chicago Theological Seminary in 1889, founded the

First Scandinavian Congregational in Chicago (Salem) and served a number of other Free Churches. He eventually settled in Minneapolis where he represented the American Bible Society. I learned to know him well. In his later retirement years, long before social security, he supplemented his income by repairing sewing machines and spent more time in our home than necessary for the repairs, much to my pleasure and gain! There is no doubt that he was influenced by Montgomery who had also spoken at the Prayer Day service in Oslo reporting on the American Congregational Church. He later encouraged Didriksen to attend the seminary in Chicago.

Another name appears in this story. Catherine Juell acted as interpreter when Montgomery spoke on Congregationalism as it was in America. He writes of her, "She was a wealthy Christian lady of that city who had travelled extensively in the U.S. Like Lydia, her heart was opened while sojourning in a foreign land, to see that a State Church is not a church after the idea of Christ and his apostles; and she is doing much for the Mission Friends who are generally from the poorer classes. She has recently given over one thousand dollars for the building of the house of worship." C. Juell was just one of the many women evangelists and teachers in the revivals. She worked with Franson as part of the evangelistic team in Denmark.[18]

On Montgomery's return to America it was "all systems go" for the Scandinavians. He was convinced that the new Mission Churches were purely congregational in polity, doctrine, liberty, and variety in unity. He insisted they were congregational to the core.

Considering that they are isolated from the world highways, are of a different language, have had no congregational missionaries sent to them, have known nothing of the Congregational Churches in any other part of the world and have thus had no help from their experiences and precedents, this similarity is very surprising. It is also gratifying to Congregationalists and instructive to students of church history to know what sort of churches have been thus self developed in another land during a time of keen public discussion of the question, "What is the New Testament idea of the true Church of Christ?" and in a time of most eager, profound, and reverent study of the Bible for light in this question, "How stands it written?" is their favorite inquiry in their determination to test all questions by the Word of God.

His conclusion was supported by both Franson and Waldenstrom. Franson, in a letter dated August 2, 1884, wrote, "these Free Churches in Scandinavia are in foundation and growth, Congregational, as you yourself know by your visit in our land." Waldenstrom in his letters had come to the same conclusion.

Montgomery's first move was to write a book on his trip and what he had learned entitled, *A Wind from the Holy Spirit in Sweden and Norway.* In it he made four recommendations as to how the Congregational Church could help the Scandinavians in America:

1. By placing the means in the treasury of the American Home Mission Society to support the Swedish, Norwegian, and Danish missionaries to preach the Gospel among their countrymen in this land.
2. By endowing two Scandinavian professorships, one in Swedish and one in Norwegian or Danish in our Theological Seminary in Chicago. These professorships should be filled by native Scandinavians.
3. By giving financial aid to the training schools for ministers at Kristenhamn and Winslof in Sweden.
4. By helping financially to start a training school for ministers in Norway or Denmark.

The world is full of men with ideas—dreamers who never seem able to make their dreams come true or turn their ideas into flesh, bone, blood and dollars. Montgomery was of a different sort. He was the right man in the right place at the right time. Prepared by his schooling for business and preaching, he first studied at the Cincinnati Business College (1858-59) and then went on to prepare for the Christian ministry at Wheaton College in 1862. During the three years there he organized the Commercial Department of the school. From Wheaton he went to Amherst, graduating in 1869. From then until 1881 he was engaged in the real estate business in Ohio. His business acumen as well as his enthusiasm is well reflected in the recommendations made following his return from the visit to Scandinavia. Like the disciples, he not only prayed for laborers for the vineyard in need of workers but was made the chief laborer by leaders of the Home Mission Society who apparently caught his vision and recognized his unique ability. One also gets the impression that he was a man able to move others to give financial support. He had already proven his organizational and administrative ability as Home Missions Superintendent for Minnesota and now he was to organize and head a new division as Superintendent of the Scandinavian Department, a position he held until his death in 1894. He also became part of the staff at the Chicago Theological Seminary to teach the immigrants English. This increased his influence as these would be the men with whom he was to work.

To make the dream come true, his first move was to help set up the Swedish Department at the Seminary in 1885. The Norwegian-Danish department, as we have reported, was organized in 1884. The second step was to place the graduates in the field. By 1886 he could report to the conference of the Congregationalists that there were already eighteen Scandinavian Home Missionaries working in nine states and one territory. Thirdly, he was able to secure the funds suggested in his recommendation for the erection of meeting houses and the support of the workers. The third oldest congregation in the former Norwegian-Danish Association is a good illustration. The congregation at Wesley, Iowa, organized in 1886 reports that its building was erected in 1887 at a cost of $1300, "including a loan on easy terms from the Congregational Union of New York" and also that "for some years the Congregational Home

Missionary Society gave financial aid toward the salary of the pastors. Of added interest is that Montgomery was present to give the dedicatory address in 1887. At this writing, plans are well under way to move the old building to the Trinity Evangelical Divinity School campus as a memorial to the pioneers in time for the Centennial in 1984. Montgomery did not confine his activities to the Central States. At the time the congregation in Jersey City, New Jersey, had its organizational meeting in 1889, Montgomery was present to give the address. Finally, he made another important contribution to the Evangelical Free Churches. In addition to his book, he wrote an article explaining the congregational system of church structure as followed in America which appeared in the papers in Sweden, Norway and the *Chicago-Bladet* in America. It was especially timely as both the *Mørgen Roden* (Morning Glow) in Norway and the *Chicago-Bladet* were preparing the believers for the organizational conferences scheduled for that very year.

Montgomery also developed a friendship with the Swedish revivalist and pastor for several years of the Swedish Tabernacle in Minneapolis, E. August Skogsberg. One early historian writes of his unique qualifications for the office of superintendent for the work of home missions among the Swedes in America.

> Montgomery was the man for the task for several reasons. First, he was an energetic and ardent friend of the Scandinavian mission people. Second, he had the confidence of and was highly respected by the Americans. Third, he had the confidence of the Scandinavian community. Fourth, he acquired a knowledge of the Swedish language as well as the work of the Scandinavian Mission Associations and the situation among the Scandinavians in general.

Montgomery passed away at the young age of fifty-five having lived a full life of service to the cause of Christ among the Scandinavians in America. By the year 1894, 105 Scandinavian congregations had joined the American Congregational Church.[19] This does not include the many others who became members of the Swedish Mission Covenant or remained independent until the formation of the Eastern and Western Districts of the Norwegian-Danish Evangelical Free Church Association.

Montgomery was succeeded by Samuel Van Santvoord Fisher (1845-1919). By the time he became superintendent in 1898, the three groups—Swedish Free, Swedish Covenant, Norwegian-Danish Free—had already formed their own denominations resulting in a diminishing role for him among the congregations within these circles. The one exception would be the Norwegian-Danish since that association was formed much later than 1884 and the Seminary continued to train leaders for the group. It was during Fisher's leadership that several of the older Norwegian and Danish congregations were formed, pastored by graduates, and subsidized by the Home Missions Society. It was also during this period that a new evangelistic thrust was made into North Dakota. Several of the congregations organized in North Dakota during that period are now part of the Evangelical Free Church of America. His name appears in the records of congregations across the United States but not as often as the name of Montgomery for obvious reasons. He was handicapped in not knowing the language, culture and life-style of the immigrants. In 1907 he returned to the pastorate.

It was inevitable that there be a change in the program of the Congregational Home Mission Society in view of the above-mentioned events. Otto C. Grauer was appointed as the successor to Fisher and served in that position with distinction until his retirement in 1930, but there was a revision of his responsibility. He was to work primarily with the Norwegians and Danes. Even during his student days at the Seminary he was hired to assist in one of the American Churches in Chicago which had a work among the Scandinavians.[20]

Grauer had one advantage over his predecessors in that he was skilled in the Norwegian language. There was also another advantage. He had taught many of the men now out in the field and he continued to serve as a teacher at the Seminary and at the successor school until 1930. He served as business manager of the Evangelisten Publishing Society during its fledgling years, on the board for the school at Rushford during the founding years and as its acting president until a permanent, full-time president (L. J. Pedersen) was installed. Even following his retirement a close contact with the Association was maintained as he served on the board of the Evangelical Alliance Mission almost from its beginning in 1891 and was the first editor of the mission's periodical, *The Broadcaster*, from 1925 to 1944. Because of the close ties of the Norwegian-Danish Association with the mission, the churches continued to enjoy his visits and his counsel until his death. His association with the mission as editor over the span of two decades, caused those of the second and third generations to not always be aware of his former position as the representative of the Congregational Home Mission Society. What is even more significant is the fact that though loyal to those for whom he worked, he never flaunted that position. Few knew that his support was coming through the courtesy and generosity of the American Congregationalists.

I was fortunate in learning to know this leader during my student days for he visited the Free Church school in Minneapolis often. During my first few years in the pastorate I met him at conferences. He had the gift of making one feel his interest in the young pastor. He walked and spoke with the dignity of a man of God.

The third contribution was in the form of direct financial aid. Many specific examples might be given. For example:

The group occupying the building, now the home of Central Free Church (pastored at one time by Princell), lost the building because they were unable to meet payments to the lumber company, etc. during the depression of 1896-97. It was through the generosity of the Congregational Church Building Society that the congregation was able to redeem the building (Swedish Temple) and adopt a new name, the Swedish Congregational Temple, 1897, and they continued as such until a merger with what is now the First Evangelical Free Church of Minneapolis in 1926.

The support was also revealed in an appeal made on behalf of Ansgar College when it was about to go under financially. A letter, addressed "to the brethren of the American Congregational Churches" called upon the Americans to help the school (1883).

Norway was also a beneficiary of the generosity. In the minutes of the annual meeting of the Norwegian sister denomination held in 1889 there is reference to a letter from Marcus Montgomery of America in which he declared that the American Congregational Church was willing to donate $5,000 toward the start of a school for workers.

The annual meeting of the Congregationalists in 1884 at Saratoga, NY, took up an offering totalling $1,141.07 toward the construction of the new meeting house in Oslo.

So we have sought to list some of the contributions of the American Congregational Church which assisted the Evangelical Free Church in its search for identity.

But there is more! It has already been noted that there was not as close a link between the Americans and the Swedish groups.

One exception which is most important to this study is that the first missionary called and sent to a field overseas was Hans J. Von Qualen, an immigrant from Denmark who was a graduate of the Chicago Theological Seminary. At his commissioning service Princell, representing the new Swedish Free Church, and Risberg of the Seminary led in the proceedings. However, there was another influence which affected people and leaders in both groups as they struggled for identity—one which may be overlooked. That was the work of Dwight L. Moody in the great spiritual revivals at that period. Stories of the campaigns were reported in both the religious and secular press in the

Scandinavian languages. But before going into the details, it would be well to mention a few dates so as to bring the events in his ministry and the search for identity into proper perspective as far as timing is concerned. Born in 1837, Moody went to Chicago at 19 and joined the Plymouth Congregational Church. At 23 he began preaching. In 1863 he organized a church following the pattern of the Congregationalists. He started what is now the Moody Bible Institute in 1886. Beginning in 1873, he and Sankey held campaigns in England, Ireland, Scotland and, of course, in America. He passed away in 1899. One historian wrote, "He traveled more than a million miles, addressed more than one hundred million persons, and personally dealt with nearly 750,000 individuals." And that was all before press agents, airplanes, fast automobiles, radio and television.

How did this all influence the Free Church founders? Keeping in mind the timing, what appealed were the following: Moody was an American revivalists blest of God. The immigrants up until that time, and some a long time later, were not sure that anything of spiritual depth could come out of the Americans. Further, he was a preaching layman. The immigrants were led by laymen! Third, he was a congregationalist who organized the church as a free and independent congregation. Finally, had not Fredrik Franson joined the church? It is of significance that when Franson organized the congregation in Denver and also the groups in Nebraska, as reported in Chapter IV, he introduced the Principles of Organization of the original Moody Church which made it possible for a local congregation to be its own denomination and be incorporated under state laws accordingly.[21]

There were also other congregationalists who had a profound influence on the Scandinavians because of their mutual interest in revivals.

Although Charles G. Finney, the evangelist, theologian and college president died in 1875, the results of his work was very much in evidence. He had also served as pastor of the Second Free Church (Congregational) and the Congregational Broadway Tabernacle both of New York City. Wherever he preached revivals prevailed. Though first a member of the Presbyterian Church and licensed to preach by that denomination he left to become a Congregationalist. His departure from certain principles of Calvinism did not go unnoticed either. Estimates of the number of converts under his ministry run as high as one-half million. With the interest the Scandinavians had in revivals the fact that Finney was a congregationalist was not lost upon them.

The same was true of another congregationalist, R. A. Torrey, who came later and served as president of the Moody Bible Institute and pastor of the Moody Church.

Having considered the contributions of the American Congregational Church, it might be of interest to share a report on the results of that stewardship by a leader who represented the Congregationalists, R. A. Jernberg, and published in 1901. It should be noted that by that date, both the Swedish Mission Church and the Swedish Free Church had been in existence sixteen to seventeen years. There were Norwegian-Danish congregations but no formal national organization. The pamphlet was apparently published to encourage further financial support from the Congregationalists. He first reviews the work of Montgomery and the developments in Sweden. The rest of the report, though repeating some facts already presented in this chapter, adds a good deal to the story by one who was there when it happened.

> In this country this Mission Covenant body numbers about one hundred and fifty churches, with a membership of more than eleven thousand. It does not include either Norwegian or Danish elements, but is wholly a Swedish Association, which from the first has been under able leadership . . . The Association has a Theological School; also a paper, *Missions Vennen*, which has a circulation of 17,500. The Swedish Mission Union by no means includes all the local churches, either in the

Home-land or in this country. Those churches which have not cared to enter into this alliance are known as the free and independent churches. Some of them are ultra in their freedom, and have little desire for a settled ministry, or even for church-organization. There is, however, a manifest tendency among them toward greater stability in church life. Of their one hundred preachers, thirty or more are in charge of definite fields. These independent churches maintain a weekly newspaper as their organ. It is the *Chicago-Bladet*, and has a circulation of 12,500. It is interesting to compare the circulation of the various church papers. The organ of the Swedish Lutheran Church has a circulation of 14,000; that of *the Missions Forbundet* a circulation of 17,500 and that of the independent churches of 12,500. Whether or not these figures are an index of the relative strength and influence of these several bodies, may be a question easier to ask than to answer, but it is not amiss to make a note of them.

Coming now to those churches, among the Swedish people in the United States, which are recognized as Congregational, we find recorded in the last Year Book about ninety, with a membership of more than six thousand. Many of these churches are not large: still there are some of considerable size, as the church in Brooklyn, with 402 members, the church in Boston with 215 members, the church in Worcester, with 351 members, that in New Britain, Conn., with 283 members, and the San Francisco church, with 230 members. These are the oldest Swedish Congregational churches in this country, but there is no reason why many of the younger churches should not equal, and surpass these mentioned in membership, if given sufficient time.

There are, then, nearly three hundred Swedish evangelical churches in this country that are either identified with us, or are so closely allied to us that our Seminary is called upon to furnish them with a trained ministry. The Swedish department of the Seminary has sent out over two hundred former students and graduates, who are scattered all over our country preaching to these churches the gospel, as they have learned it in Chicago Theological Seminary. Some, even of the less conservative Lutheran churches are availing themselves of the services of ministers trained in this school. Among the Danes and Norwegians the work of our denomination has been slower, and not of so vigorous growth as among the Swedes. The reason for this is that there has not been the religious upheaval in Norway and Denmark that there has been in Sweden: and whatever results we are able to show in this Danish-Norwegian work are due almost entirely to the work of our Home Missionary Society among these nationalities.

Our Seminary is really the pioneer in this work, for it opened its Danish-Norwegian department in 1884, while the oldest Norwegian Congregational church recorded in our Year Book, that in Boston, was not organized until 1885: and it is not too much to say, that during all the subsequent years the Seminary has been the rallying point for all this work, and has been largely instrumental in its permanent establishment. One hundred young men have gone out from this department of the Seminary. Our Western Association of Norwegian Congregational Churches was organized here: and our Norwegian church paper *Evangelisten*, was been published from the Seminary, for the most part under the management of the Norwegian professors, since its beginning in 1889.

As a result of our missionary labors among the Danes and Norwegians, we have now more than twenty organized churches with a membership exceeding a thousand. Besides these there are twenty or thirty other churches, not in formal association with us, but so closely allied to us, that they welcome our missionaries and students both as occasional and permanent supplies, and generally recognize our paper, *Evangelisten*, as their representative. These churches are strictly independent, having no church association, and are in some respects similar to the Swedish independent churches already mentioned.

The Scandinavian department of Carleton College, under the care of one of the first and most earnest laborers in our home missionary field, which he left only at the imperative demand of the educational work, has grown in strength and importance, and has made no inconsiderable contribution to the general work.

Besides the regularly organized church work, with its associations, church papers, and educational departments, another powerful religious agency has been set in motion, at least in part, as a result of our Scandinavian work. This is a foreign missionary society, The Scandinavian Alliance Mission, almost entirely supported by the churches here described, and maintaining no less than eighty-five missionaries in heathen lands. This society, of which our Swedish professor, Rev. Fridolf Risberg, is the honored secretary and treasurer, expends annually about $25,000 in its work for Africa, India, China and Japan.

A general survey of the work which the Congregationalists have been doing among the Scandinavians would be incomplete without the grateful acknowledgment of the good offices and generous help of the Church Building Society.

Sometimes the wisdom of this foreign home-missionary work is questioned, and the critics ask: "Does it pay?" Let us look at the question from a purely financial standpoint, as far as this is possible. Let us leave out all thought of the indirect influence exerted by our work among the Scandinavians. Let us say nothing about the 200 Swedish Free churches in this country, with fifteen thousand members, and the 100 Norwegian Free churches, with 6,000 members, all of whom stand in a very different, and much more friendly, relation to us than to any other denomination. Let us confine ourselves to the seventeen years of work, which we have done among the Scandinavians, and compare them with the results of the other home missionary work of our denomination. The Scandinavian work has cost about $12,000 annually. This is two per cent of the $600,000 expended every year by our churches,through the Home Missionary Society and its auxiliaries. As a result we have 110 Scandinavian Congregational churches, with a membership of 7,000. If the aggregate result of all the work done by the Home Missionary Society alone had been on the same scale, we should have had an increase of churches, during the last seventeen years, of 5,500, with a membership of 350,000.

It would seem, therefore, that the work of our Home Missionary Society among the Scandinavian population of our country is the most economical work it is doing, yielding the largest results for the least expenditure of money in the present, and laying foundations of strong churches in the future, when the parents shall have given place to the children, who to-day are introduced to the history and polity of the Pilgrim faith through the work now done for them. Without this work they would remain aliens in spirit and thought, for another generation, and be lost altogether to our churches at last, and very likely also to the kingdom of our Lord.[22]

There is one additional influence we will consider before

we follow the pioneers as they finally put the pieces together and that is the role played by the periodicals in the search for identity.

FOOTNOTES—CHAPTER V

1. Karl Olsson, *By One Spirit*, Chicago, The Covenant Press, 1962, p. 336.
2. After the Norwegian School was moved from Rushford, Minnesota to Minneapolis, the hospitality circle in my home was enlarged to include students. I learned early that preachers were great story tellers and many students, once relaxed, were pranksters. Their homes were thousands of miles away, so mine became a second home. As to preachers, they had another reason for coming, in addition to a good Norwegian-style meal. I was a mimic of the men in the pulpit. I've been told and do remember being placed on a chair or table to "preach like so and so." It became a game, at times, to guess who was the victim, at the moment, of the imitation. There were no nurseries or little tots' rooms in the church in those days. Mother was on one side of the pulpit singing in the "stringband," and father on the other side singing in the choir. My brother and I were placed in center on the first pew where all three, including the man in the pulpit, could watch us. Then there were also the hundreds of eyes behind us. I have been told I was well behaved in church! As to mimicry, the greater the idiosyncracy, and there were many, the better the imitation!
3. From the introduction to the reprint in 1960 of Williston Walker, *The Creeds and Platforms of Congregationalism*, Boslow, Pilgrim Press, 1893, by Douglas Horton, p. XIII.
4. From the Cambridge Platform, 1648, para. XII.
5. Walker, op. cit., p. 583
6. This is also true of the Doctrinal Statement of the Evangelical Free Church of America.
7. Walker, op. cit., p. 576
8. Nelson, A. P., *Puritanernas och Pilgrimernas Historia*, Pilgrim Press, Boston, 1901, p. 327
9. Olsson, Karl, op. cit., p. 316
10. Fridolf Risberg may be better known among the immediate past and present generations for his connections with The Evangelical Alliance Mission. He served as a member of the board and as treasurer. his final request was that he be buried next to his close friend and associate, Fredrick Franson, a request which was honored. The Mission erected the Franson-Risberg building in Chicago in their memory.
11. Olsson, Karl, op. cit., p. 388
12. Based on information provided by Manfred Waldemar Kohl, *Congregationalism in America*, Oak Creek, Wisconsin, The Congregational Press, 1977, p. 37.
13. The name George Wiberg is of special interest. It reveals that there was some contact with the leaders in the Ansgar Synod at that time. As a student he was the instrument of revivals in Maine (1874) and also preached in a number of other Eastern states. He served as pastor of an Ansgar congregation in Wooster, Mass; was a member of the committee seeking a merger with the Mission Synod in 1879; and his name appears in the minutes of the first conference following the meeting in Boone in 1884, namely at the

American Congregational Church, Minneapolis, March 1885. He was later appointed a general home missionary for Minnesota to preach among the Swedish Free churches which could not support a pastor.

14. The immigrants of the last 30 years are of a different sort. They might better be called sojourners as their purpose is not to settle down but to put in a minimum of ten years so as to qualify for Social Security; then return to Scandinavia and in due time collect on the Social Security pensions from America. Without establishing roots in America these were not the best material for founding new churches. Those who were believers settled temporarily in areas where there were churches still using the mother tongue (especially in Brooklyn and Chicago). There they were spectators rather than participants.

15. Montgomery, Marcus, *A Wind From the Holy Spirit in Sweden and Norway*, New York, American Home Mission Society, 1884, pp. 6, 7

16. *Ibid.*, p. 18

17. Based on an article by Bror Walan, "Americanen Som Upptackte Svenska Missionsforbundet," in *Vinterny*, 1963, Christmas number, Stockholm, Missions Forbundets Forlag, p. 12

18. Montgomery, op. cit., p. 24. For further information on C. Juell, see *A Woman of Her Times* by Della Olson.

19. Nelson, A. P., op. cit., pp. 315, 316

20. Frederick E. Emrick, pastor of the church in which Grauer assisted was another generous supporter of the Norwegian-Danish immigrants. As pastor of the Tabernacle Congregational Church in Chicago, he opened the doors of the church to the Norwegians and Danes to conduct services under the leadership of P. C. Trandberg. He promoted the establishment of the Norwegian-Danish Department at the Chicago Theological Seminary under the early leadership of Trandberg and was also on the committee which approached the Swedes in 1885 to make a similar offer of a department at the school.

21. Moody's Modus Operandi was also familiar to the believers in the Scandinavian countries. When Waldenstrom, in the discussions leading up to the formation of the Covenant in Sweden in 1878, defended his opposition to a creedal position, he used Moody as an example of how God also blesses a non-confessional layman.

22. Jernberg, R. A., From an eight-page tract published by the Congregational Home Mission Society in New York, 1901 entitled *Scandinavian Congregationalism in America*.

Chapter VI

PRESSING ON

Waldenstrom's often repeated question, *Huru staar det skrevet?* (where stands it written?) became the slogan of challenge during the period leading up to and following the founding of the sister "Free" denominations in the three countries of Scandinavia (Swedish-1878; Norwegian-1884; Danish-1888).[1]

However, the movements were not only a result of a return to the Scriptures but also a result of the power of the press. The congregations, as so well expressed in the Diamond Jubilee Story,[2] were but "isolated outposts." There were great distances to cover between them. There were no automobiles; no telephones; no radios; no televisions; no airplanes. The first telephone switchboard was set up in New Haven, Connecticut, in 1878 with only 21 subscribers. Though an experimental first steam engine automobile was built in France in 1870, mass production of the gasoline automobile engine didn't begin until after the turn of the century. E. A. Halleen used to boast that he was the first pastor in the whole city of Minneapolis to own a car!

But the pioneers had two things going for them. The first was the development of printing from moveable type, generally attributed to Johann Gutenberg of Germany, and first used to print the indulgences (1454-55) and the Latin Vulgate Bible (1456). There was behind our pioneers four hundred years of constant improvement in the techniques of printing, thus speeding up the process and lowering the cost of making the Bible available to the common people and making it possible to mass produce periodicals. The second is somewhat ironic in Scandinavia. The government postal systems would deliver these periodicals which often attacked the church-state system—the very government for which the postmen were working. In America the mail service delivered the papers from Scandinavia and those published in the United States to the outposts from coast to coast so that the groups were not completely isolated nor were they uninformed.

The interesting fact is that while most organizations, religious or secular, start publishing promotional papers, magazines, etc. after they have come into existence, the five publications to be discussed were begun before the birth of the denominations. It is not without great significance that four out of five were published and edited by outstanding laymen. All were published privately and owned by these men. After all, there were no denominations to engage in a publishing business. So it can be said, even in that connection, that the movements were truly called, *Laesare Bevegelser* (readers' movements) led by laymen!

Then, to use a military term, they were the "advance parties" in the march toward the freedom and independence of the churches.

The first was Sweden's *Pietisten* (The Pietist) started by

George Scott in 1842 and edited by Karl Olof Rosenius (1816-1868) from 1842 to 1868 and upon his death, by Paul Peter Waldenstrom (1838-1917) until his death in 1917.

Rosenius, son of a Lutheran State Church minister, was brought up in what was then revival country in northern Sweden. He dropped out of the university before completing his studies and from then on gave all his talents and time to the readers' movement. The paper contained devotional messages and during his editorship did not openly attack the State church, though he defied the rules of the church in his practice. He, along with others, was engaged in an abortive attempt to reform the religious life of the country. He remained a layman all his life. His message was that salvation, forgiveness of sin, was not by human merit or through some act or acts of the church but through the unmerited grace of God. As a preacher, he went against the establishment in his approach to evangelism. The services were conventicals (a meeting or assembly for religious worship, especially a secret or illicit one). Karl Olsson summarized what the conventical meant as viewed from the position of the State Church. (1) It was a violation of the office of the church in that only trained and ordained clergymen were a trustworthy source of truth. (2) It was a violation of the position of the church as to the right place of worship which, outside of family worship in the home, was restricted to church buildings. (3) It was a violation of the prescribed form of worship. "It was not held at the usual hours; did not use the liturgy, vestments, etc." (4) It violated the sanctity of the social structure since it tended to put into places of spiritual leadership those whose social and intellectual status was not up to the "proper" level.[3]

Great though the influence of Rosenius was as a preacher, it was as a writer that, by the Holy Spirit, he moved the greater number. An indication of the disturbing influence of Pietisten to the establishment is indicated in the published warning against the reading of the Rosenius paper which "contains heresy and those who accept such teachings will miss the way to heaven and downgrade divine grace to the level of licentiousness."

Ollen writes of him as the trailblazer of the laymen's work in Sweden.[4] David Nyvall pays a beautiful tribute to him: "He published and edited for many years a periodical called *Pietisten,* unique in power and read by people in most of the Scandinavian countries and in America. And yet his greatest work was not even the publishing of this journal but his correspondence by which he became the pastor and spiritual advisor of a nation. Unassuming as he was and well aware of his limitations, by strength of character and practical leadership he became a national power and creator of a new order of things."[5]

Another historian writes that the object Rosenius had with the publication of *Pietisten* was to "lead Christians to a deeper knowledge of Bible truths and to guide them in matters pertaining to the spiritual life . . . Through the magazine he became an influential leader among the Christians in Sweden. Few men have ever been held in higher esteem by the religious element in Sweden than C. O. Rosenius, and very few men have so well deserved the confidence he thus enjoyed."[6]

Westin notes that the influence of Rosenius and Waldenstrom also had its effect on the Free Church movement of Norway.[7]

Following the death of Rosenius, Waldenstrom took over as editor and the paper became more militant, resulting in the open break with the Lutheran State Church and the formation of the Swedish Covenant. During his editorship the paper became even stronger and more popular. One of the great and divisive controversies on both sides of the ocean during the latter part of the century and well into the 1900s was Waldenstrom's theory of the atonement which he published in 1872 but never preached as a sermon. This raised a storm of protest in the church. We cite this as an illustration of the power of the periodical without getting into the controversy itself.

In Norway the paper was *Morgenrøden* (Morning Glow) edited by Carl Bernhard Falck (1834-1919). Brandeland writes that though the Free Church of Norway was not organized until 1884, there was a fellowship known as the United Society for the Free Mission Societies.[8] It was at a meeting of a few of these societies which assembled in Oslo in 1883 that the decision was made to try and form an organization. It is interesting to read that Princell was present and took part in the discussions at this meeting which agreed to publish the paper. Much of its success was due to the dedication and skills of the editor.

Falck deserves a larger place in the history of the work among the Norwegians and Danes than he is given. Many know of Rosenius and Waldenstrom, but who is Falck?

He started as a school teacher at the age of 31 but because he had left the State Church to cast his lot with the free fellowship (Lammers Revival) he could no longer continue. He became a merchant in his secular life and chairman of the local group in the fellowship at Skien where the revival under Lammers had started and where the latter, as the minister in the State Church, withdrew along with many members.

A magazine published later by the organization after 1884, writes of Falck as the frontline trailblazer in his writing and preaching. His handling of the various questions about doctrine, the Biblical principles for the organization of the local congregations and the larger association revealed him to be an alert, zealous and productive founder. He also mastered the German, English, Hebrew, and Greek languages. Before being asked to edit the new paper, he served as a *reisepredikant* (itinerant preacher or home missionary) for the independent groups formed as a result of the Lammers' revival. Hearing about the revivals in Sweden under the leadership of Franson, Falck went to the neighboring country to study his work and invited him to Norway—an invitation which was accepted. The results of Franson's arrival on January 1, 1883, marked the beginning of what is now the Norwegian Mission Covenant. Falck, in addition to his editorial responsibilities, wrote several books and pamphlets on such subjects as "A true and false holiness," "The Scriptures and Pietism," "Election," "Is Jesus the true God?"[9]

He was a true churchman as evidenced by his election to the first executive committee of the new denomination.

Falck was also a statesman. On three occasions during the political crisis in 1895 he was called upon for counsel by the Prime Minister of Norway. He fought for the political as well as the religious freedom of his country. One reporter wrote that when the Norwegian flag was raised for the first time over Akerhus on June 7, 1905, Falck stood and wept for joy.

It was through *Morgenrøden* that the call was issued to the Christian Mission Societies and congregations in Norway to attend a constitutional convention. The call also included a proposed twelve-point statement as to name, purpose, and polity. This was announced in March of 1884 and the first convention convened on July 8, the same year.[10]

A recent letter adds emphasis to the influence of *Morgenrøden* and Falck on the birth of the Norwegian "Free Church."

As to the written word in periodicals, I do think that they have been very important in the promotion of the fellowship between free church belivers and in the organization of our movement. The Lammers' revival from 1856 got a periodical appearing once a month from 1859 to 1960. This Lammers did with the periodical of the Swiss Evangelical Free Church in mind and as a source of inspiration. As far as I can see this was a real tie between all the Lammers' churches, later on called Free Mission, that called Fredrik Franson to Norway.

Just after the great revivals in the Lammers' churches broke out with Fredrik Franson as the tool of the Lord, the paper *Morgenrøden* was founded with C. B. Falck, the national secretary of the Lammers' churches, as editor. And as I read *Morgenrøden* I think this is the most important thing in the development from the Lammers Free Mission to the organization of Det Norske Misjonsforbund in 1884. At once when they wrote about it in the paper, proposals came from the board of the Free Mission, everything was lined up and were apt and worked well. It is really true as you say that the paper became the vehicle by which the meeting in 1884 was promoted. Then the periodicals were filled with articles about the formation of our denomination.[12]

Denmark, because of the ties between the two countries, was influenced by the revivals and leaders of the free movements in Norway.[11]

In Denmark it was *Pilgrimen* (the Pilgrim) published and edited by Mogens Abraham Sommers (B. 1829). Sommers, though not among the founders of the Danish Mission Covenant in 1888, nevertheless broke the ground. Born of Jewish parents, he grew up under the influence of a bitterness against the state church clergy in the heart of his father (anti-semitism). He was converted on Good Friday, 1849, and became a school teacher in 1852 having outstanding success. An admirer of Søren Kierkegaard, an outspoken adversary of the religious establishment, he met with the controversial theologian in 1854-55 and was influenced greatly by him. Resigning from the teaching profession after four years, he became a lay preacher. During the same year he went to Norway to meet with Lammers who ordained him as a pastor for the free apostolic congregations in Denmark, an ordination which was later withdrawn following a break with Lammers. Sommers was another one of the leading revivalists of that period. Many of the converts, under his influence and through his championing the cause of religious freedom and the right of local groups of believers to form independent congregations, were ready to join the Mission Covenant congregations during the 1880-1890 period.

Though *Pilgrimen* was published for a brief time, forty weeks from October 1859 to July 1860, the influence of the editor as an evangelist lasted much longer. A recent letter from the Moderator of the Danish Mission Covenant supports this conclusion:

107

There seems to have been several connections between "The Sommer Movement" beginning in 1853 and ending about 1876, when Mogens Abraham Sommers emigrated to USA, and the Danish Covenant Church founded 12 years later. Some of the free evangelical congregations which were formed one or two decades after were established in towns and areas where M. A. Sommer had formerly worked and preached. Here the soil obviously was prepared for a free evangelical movement. Here were still people who remembered Sommers tough fight with The Lutheran State Church and its priests. These people—even not appreciating Sommers methods—were in many ways prepared for the evangelical revivals that appeared in Jutland as well as in Copenhagen and the Northern part of Zealand.[13]

Before turning to the two periodicals in America a reminder may be in order. First, we read and hear a good deal about how the churches and the denominations (Norwegian-Danish and Swedish) in America were born in the time of spiritual revival. We should also thank our heavenly Father for those periodicals which were born in the same revivals and were the harbingers of a new springtime after the dark winters of the previous centuries. One might wonder why so much space is occupied with the papers in Scandinavia when we are dealing with the search for identity in the United States. The answer should be obvious. The immigrants, many of them, were familiar with the periodicals before they emigrated to America and some even subscribed to them after arriving on the new shores. Further, the struggles for religious freedom and the pattern of the new congregations of believers as recorded in the papers assisted the pioneers in reaching their conclusions.

Chicago-Bladet (Chicago Paper) was first published on February 16, 1877, at the very time the future of the Ansgar and Mission Synods was being debated. Just as the three papers already reported on, it was independently owned and edited by a layman who, like the others, was not only a gifted writer but a revival preacher. John Martenson learned the trade of typesetting in Sweden and for about ten years following his move to America worked for a number of newspapers in the Chicago area, including the writing of persuasive articles, not necessarily on religious subjects. His life changed directions when converted under the preaching of Erik August Skogsberg. The latter was preaching to great crowds of Swedes in the same meeting place as did Moody and with his full support in 1876. As a result he was called the "Swedish Moody." Skosberg's name appears often in the early history. An independent at heart, he was closer to the Mission Synod than the other, but sought to bring the two together. Skogsberg, in his memoirs, tells the story of the burden upon the heart of Martenson following his conversion. "He came to me to seek counsel as to what I thought about his burden for publishing a small newspaper and if I would go along with the idea. I answered that I saw it would be beneficial for the work and although I could not give financial aid, I would provide moral support and good will as my time permits. We agreed to proceed and soon thereafter the first issue of *Chicago-Bladet* made its appearance."[14]

In 1878 Martenson purchased and absorbed another Swedish paper, *Sion's Baner* (Zion's Banner). When the Ansgar Synod was dissolved in 1884 and the School in Illinois given over to the community, he secured the services of Princell, its president, as assistant editor.

The paper promised that the contents would be based on nothing but the Scripture, not on any particular church denomination, "for we are firm in our conviction that no one attains blessedness because he is a member of this or that denomination but only by belonging to Jesus and having forgiveness through faith in Him." He also promised not to foster division among the believers on the basis of denominational affiliation. However, in his and Princell's crusade for the independence of the local churches, opposition to all forms of authority over the churches got the upper hand. This divided the believers. The crusade resulted in unfortunate divisions and must have been displeasing to the Holy Spirit. There were charges and counter charges.

There was much more in the statement of purpose than the declaration of its religious position. This statement appeared on the first page (upper left-hand corner, one column in length) of the first issue, February 15, 1977, and in the same spot in every issue through June of that year. He wrote that he had taken upon himself, with the promised support of Skogsberg—his father in the faith—to publish a paper in the belief that a genuine Christian newspaper in Swedish was needful in America. One newspaper after another has appeared, all claiming to inform the public truthfully about current events but, according to Martenson, not one mentions the most important information of all—the need for personal salvation from sin and to be in the right relationship with Jesus Christ. The religious purpose is hereby stated. However, it was also going to be a political paper. In politics it would follow, in general, the principles of the Republicans though not so blindly as to say "yes and amen" to everything they proposed. Candidates for political office would be supported solely on the basis of qualifications for the office sought.

It is interesting and significant to note that all of the five papers were involved in the main stream of the life of the nations concerned. In the Scandinavian countries it was natural since in opposition to the policies of the religious establishments they could not but criticize the government that controlled them and appointed their leaders.

The early issues published many sermons by Moody and Waldenstrom in full, giving additional support to the claim made in previous as well as following chapters of the influence these men had on the thinking of the Scandinavian immigrants.

The issues in 1878 reported, over several month's time, the discussions in Sweden which led to the founding of the Covenant of Sweden that year. The Swedes in America were thus well informed and prepared for the discussions leading up to the decisions of 1884 and 1885.

From this position, in the point of time, I have the impression that *Chicago-Bladet* was not only responsible for the founding of the Swedish Free Church but contributed also to the formation of the Swedish Covenant, though some of my Covenant friends will strongly disagree. But the more Martenson and Princell promoted the independence of the local church and a national organization composed of delegates and pastors rather than member churches, the more those holding the latter view had to study church polity and the more they were convinced they were right and the *Chicago-Bladet* wrong. This does not mean that the Covenant came into existence as a reaction but the arguments became a catalyst leading to the events of 1885.

Minnesskrift writes of Martenson that he made his paper an organ for studies in the Bible. He was an admirer of Waldenstrom's interpretation of the atonement, a zealous agitator for the authority of the local congregation as the highest authority next to the Bible itself, and an enthusiastic student and exponent of prophecy, particularly pertaining to the second coming of Jesus Christ.[15]

Princell found in *Chicago-Bladet* the vehicle for spreading his view on church polity as well as other doctrines. With great skill he marshalled his arguments in favor of an association which would provide local freedom; and with a powerful vocabulary he wrote against all forms of denominationalism, accusing them of being a work which separated believers within God's congregation.[16]

The Swedish Free Church held him in high esteem and considered him as one, if not the, founder. It is only fair to note that others, equally as dedicated to searching the Scriptures for clues regarding church polity, while admiring his skill in oratory and with the pen, his broad knowledge of the Scriptures and of history, would not have been willing to place him on a pedestal or put a halo about his head.

He emphasized this (his opinions) very strongly without due regard to the brethren who differed with him in these matters.[17]

His campaign against denominationalism began following his expulsion from the Lutheran Ministerial and several years before becoming editor:

> To Illinois Princell came in 1880, and took up at once his propaganda against denominations as something in his opinion as not only unscriptural but a most heinous evil, amounting to spiritual prostitution. His propaganda resulted in the voluntary secession from the Mission Synod of at least three congregations.[18]

> His insistence upon the independence of the local church now became not only a theory but a fervent practice. In this report, Princell was a maimed man . . . Princell was a devoted spirit with considerable, if miscellaneous, erudition. He was a talented preacher who now and then attained the level of golden eloquence. He was an inspiring leader even though he had little administrative skill. But he was, unfortunately, a man with an *idee fixe*, an obsessive aversion to denominational structure—an obsession which made him dangerous to the enterprise of uniting the Mission Friends and gives him the distinction of fathering the Evangelical Free Church and much of the travail which signaled its birth.[19]

There is another dimension of this remarkable man as revealed in his reply to the charges made against him by the Lutheran Ministerial. See footnote.[20]

The contribution of *Chicago-Bladet* to the birth and development of the Swedish Free Church was well put by a man who knew, probably better than anyone, its history and value to the church. Roy Thompson wrote in the *Diamond Jubilee Story:* [21]

> The Swedish Evangelical Free Church is a striking example of the power of the printed page. It is inconceivable that any such movement as The Evangelical Free Church could have existed apart from the influence of Chicago-Bladet, the Swedish Christian newspaper edited and published by John Martenson of Chicago. This influential paper, from the very beginning of its publication, was the voice and champion and unofficial organ of those who eventually associated themselves in the work of the Swedish Evangelical Free Church of America. The spirit of independence so vigorously

advocated and promoted by Chicago-Bladet became the spirit of those Christians and those Christian churches that looked to Chicago-Bladet for spiritual guidance. The constituency of Chicago-Bladet became the constituency of The Swedish Evangelical Free Church. The beliefs and convictions that dominated the thinking of our Free Church people were the result, to a large extent, of the molding influence of John Martenson's Chicago-Bladet.[22]

The story of the Norwegian-Danish paper, *Evangelisten* (The Evangelist) varies just a little from the other four in that it was not founded and edited by a layman. It started publication in 1889 with Jernberg as editor and Dyrness, a student at the seminary, as his assistant. Other students at the seminary assisted in its composition, printing, and mailing which was done in part at the seminary's expense.

Once again we have an example of the generosity of the American Congregationalists. In addition to the help at the seminary the Home Mission Societies provided an annual financial subsidy during the paper's first decade of existence.

Montgomery was a prime mover for a paper for the Norwegians. In 1887 he reported, "Among the Norwegians, the work moves forward slowly but hopefully. The overshadowing need in this direction is a newspaper in the Norwegian-Danish language, to make known among these people that Congregational Churches are founded upon the simple and peaceful principles of the New Testament." Montgomery as superintendent for the work among the Scandinavians made several appeals to the constituency for help, typical of which was the one published the year the new publication was launched.

> Our Norwegian missionaries have long been calling for a religious paper for their people in their own language, and saying that it would do more good than twenty missionaries on the field. They now say that such a paper is a necessity, and we are making an effort to meet this need. The paper is called *Evangelisten*, and is issued semimonthly in Chicago at 60 cents per annum; in clubs at 50 cents per annum. Professor

Reinart A. Jernberg of our Chicago Theological Seminary has taken on an extra burden without any compensation. The Congregational Sunday School and Publishing Society has kindly come to its aid in a financial grant.

But beside these helps, the paper must have at least 1500 paying subscribers to get through its first year without debt. . . . We now ask that individuals, churches, and Sunday schools, willing to have a share in this religious paper for two nationalities, will send in their clubs subscriptions. Such papers will be mailed to Norwegian and Danish families on the frontier.

The appeal was also signed by a representative for the Congregational Sunday Schools and Publishing Society and appeared in a number of publications.

In retrospect, one may be surprised to discover that not all agreed that such a paper "would do more good than twenty missionaries." There was much opposition to the use of home mission funds by the American Society to subsidize a magazine. The paper itself was attacked by other Scandinavian religious periodicals for misuse of missionary money!

Jernberg resigned as editor in 1899. The Norwegians and Danes, still not organized into a national association, could not take over the paper so a corporation was formed known as the Evangelisten Publishing Society with investors buying stock at ten dollars a share. It was given to the Norwegian-Danish Free Church in 1919 through Dyrness, then the chairman of the Board for the Publishing Society.

Upon the resignation of Jernberg and the placing of publication in the hands of the Society, Dyrness became the editor serving for the first two years. Olai Urang notes that "Dyrness was a strong and forthright editor, not afraid to express his opinion or to fight back against unjust criticism."[23]

Grauer accepted responsibility as business manager and served in that capacity from 1899 to 1907.

Thompson also writes of the role played by the paper in

114

the birth of the district and national assocation:

> The Norwegian-Danish Evangelical Free Church movement did not stem from an organization on either side of the ocean. Individuals who saw a need gathered the believers together and started small missions or churches. These groups were independent of other such groups and in many cases even ignorant of the existence of these other churches. It was not until the Scandinavian publication, *Evangelisten* began to find its way into the homes of Free Church people that there was much of an attempt to unite about anything. But, significantly, the *Evangelisten* of May 22, 1891, went so far as to propose a model constitution for Free Churches.[24]

> The *Evangelisten* was destined to be a unifying medium for people all over the land. As such its influence cannot be overestimated.[25]

Thompson summarized it well in an address to the Jubilee Conference on the subject, *"The Evangelical Free Church and the Printed Page"*:

> What *Chicago-Bladet* did for the Swedish Evangelical Free Church, *Evangelisten* did for the Norwegian-Danish Evangelical Free Church. Mr. Urang points out in the *Diamond Jubilee Story* that during the first few years the movement consisted of a group of "isolated" outposts where immigrants who had found the Lord in the old country revivals gathered together for fellowship and service of their Lord. The influence of *Evangelisten* is seen in the fact that within two years after its inception, the Western Association was organized in September of 1891 and the Eastern Association organized later in the same year.

> I want to point out that the Evangelical Free Church of America owes its very existence to the printed page; that the principles and ideals on which it was established have been preserved and perpetuated by the printed page.[26]

Support for the claim that the periodical was and is essential to the denomination also comes from a wholly unexpected source. In 1962 the denominational headquarters protested the levying of state property taxes for the years 1960, 61, 62. My argument was that paper for the *Beacon*, for example, was here today and gone tomorrow. An assessor could happen to be present right after the delivery and just before it was made into *Beacons*. The protest also declared that the publishing of magazines, papers and books was absolutely essential to our existence as a denomination since under our congregational system there was no control of the churches by a bishop, board of elders, or other. Leaders could only provide guidance through information and inspiration. The District Court of the Fourth Judicial District, State of Minnesota, ruled in favor of the denomination and also filed the following memorandum:

> Practically all of the output of the Free Church Press consists of books, pamphlets, periodicals, or other literature, reflecting the religious views of the Evangelical Free Church of America, Inc., and those of other religious organizations and individuals adhering to identical or similar religious beliefs. Practically all of the sales of the Beacon Book Store are sales of such literature. Because of the free and autonomous or semi-autonomous structure of individual churches adhering to the Evangelical Free Church of America, Inc., the publication and dissemination of such literature is the primary method of holding the denomination together and obtaining doctrinal agreement and solidarity. The output and sales of both the Press and the Store are either religious *and* denominational or simply religious in character, for member churches, their members, members of other churches, and other individuals of like belief.

We are about to come to the end of the search for identity. That identity has now become clear. Next we will try to put it all together—how everything fell or was pushed (?) into place.

FOOTNOTES—CHAPTER VI

1. Ollen, N. P., *Paul Peter Waldenstrom, en Levnadstekning*, Svenska Missions Forbundets Forlag, Stockholm, 1917, pg. 69.
2. *Diamond Jubilee Story*, Free Church Publications, Minneapolis 1959, p. 67.
3. Olsson, Karl, op. cit., p. 53.
4. Ollen, N. P., op. cit., p. 21.

5. Nyvall, David, *The Swedish Covenanters,* Covenant Press, Chicago, 1954, p. 25.
6. Bowman, C. V., *The Mission Covenant of America,* Covenant Book Concern, Chicago, 1925, p. 13.
7. Westin, Gunnar, *The Free Church Through the Ages,* Broadman Press, Nashville, 1954, p. 356.
8. This Society was a forerunner to the Mission Covenant of Norway.
9. Braendeland, Daniel, *Det Norskemission-Forbund gjennen femty ar,* Det Norske Missions Forbunds Forlag, Drammen, Norway, 1934, p. 16
10. *Missionsbladet,* Number 17, 1890 written by C. H. Henricksen.
11. Diesen, Ingulf, Det Norske Missions Forbund Histori. An unpublished manuscript written in 1971 by the head of the denomination in Norway which provided much of the material on Falck.
12. In a personal letter from Dr. Ingulf Diesen, head of the church in Norway, dated May 22, 1979.
13. In a personal letter from "Overdyrlaege" Helge Rasmussen, Moderator of the Church in Denmark, dated June 3, 1979. The Danish Evangelical Covenant was organized in 1888.
14. Skogsberg, E. August, *Minnen och Upplevelser,* Veckobladets Trykeri, Minneapolis, 1915, p. 155, 156.
15. *Minneskrift,* published in commemoration of the thirtieth anniversary of the Swedish Free Church in 1914, p. 18.
16. *Ibid.,* p. 7
17. Bowman, op. cit., p. 141
18. Nyvall, op. cit., p. 51
19. Olsson, op. cit., p. 248
20. Quotes in *Levnadsminnen* by Josephine Princell and translated from S w e d i s h .
After answering a list of questions put to him by the Ministerial, he concludes: (page 46)
"The above, my esteemed and beloved brethren, is my answer to the question that was put to me, and my explanation of my present views on these important subjects, stated as briefly and concisely as I can do it in the short time I have had. Let me add: I am only a weak, short-sighted and fallible person, no one can feel that any more than I can. I may have misconstrued in some or in all points the immeasurable and unsearchable subject referred to here. If, now that these subjects have been so widely considered at this meeting both privately and publicly, you will, as I humbly pray, grant me reasonable time for further prayer, thought, and humble study of God's Word, then, if I find that I am wrong in any or all of it, I shall with all my heart take it back."
21. Thompson, Roy A. served for many years as editor for Free Church Publications—first as editor of the Young People's Messenger (1921-26), second as editor of *Chicago-Bladet* for another five years, third as editor of *The Evangelical Beacon* from 1931—1958 and secretary of Publications until his retirement in 1964.
22. *The Diamond Jubilee Story,* op. cit., p. 128
23. *Ibid.,* p. 80
24. *Ibid.,* p. 79
25. *Ibid.,* p. 71
26. *Forward in the Faith of our Fathers.* Messages delivered at the Diamond Jubilee Conference of the Evangelical Free Church of America at Denver, Colorado, June 22-28, 1959, p. 104.

Chapter VII

PUTTING IT ALL TOGETHER

By the time we reach the historic year of 1884, the idea of a local fellowship of believers being organized along congregational lines was generally accepted although not necessarily formally adopted by all the groups existing at that time. There were only about a half dozen communities of believers represented at the Boone meeting that were organized and most of these were patterned after the congregational structure of the Moody Church in Chicago. However, in most places, whatever minimum of structure existed was very informal.

As the Golden Jubilee book reports: "The churches that were organized in those days were independent. They were proud of the fact . . . To begin with, the churches could hardly be called organized congregations. No records were kept, no constitutions were adopted; no prescribed methods of work were followed. Their prevailing ambition was to stay clear of denominationalism. They were afraid to be connected with any denomination. As a matter of fact, there are a considerable number who to this day (1934) maintain that the organization is not and can never be a denomination in the general sense of the word. These contend that the Free Church constitutes only an affiliation of local, independent churches for the sole purpose of propagating missionary work at home and abroad."[1] There was even an aversion to having resident pastors. Halleen writes that when he entered the work ten years after it was organized there were only two or three churches in the entire state of Minnesota that had resident pastors. The rest were served by itinerant preachers who usually traveled in pairs. The local work was led by a layman who was called, in most cases, elder. To them an elder, in what they considered the New Testament sense, was another name for pastor, teacher, overseer, etc. But since he was not ordained (neither were many of the others, for that matter) the name of pastor was not applied. Later, when pastors were called and installed, limitations were placed on their authority over the affairs of the congregations.

Authority rested in the congregation, not the pastor. This was true whether the minister was a man or, as in a few cases, a woman. One of the oldest congregations—Denver, 1880—reveals what was a common attitude in the early days. In the section on pastor, the constitution declares: "This church recognizes and emphasizes the rights and duties of all Christian believers to proclaim the virtues of Christ according to their respective ability and divine gifts from God, but for the welfare of the work within the Church it is deemed advisable and practicable for the members of the church to call a pastor. The pastor shall preach the Word of God, lead the devotional services of the church, visit the sick and needy, and carefully attend to the matter of imparting instruction in the Holy Scriptures to the children and young people. He shall further keep a record of members received and discharged, issue church letters to those who desire, and conduct all other activities associated with his calling. He shall give a report of the condition of the church at the annual business meeting."

The Norwegian-Danish history is not exactly identical.

By the time the Eastern and Western Districts were merged in 1912, the local pattern was quite well established. This was due, in a large part, to the influence of the seminary. Those who were not served by resident pastors were visited by home missionaries supported by the Home Missions Society of the American Congregational Church. But, the same fears of too much organization is apparent from the records of the beginning years. One of the early evangelists, in his autobiography, writes in reference to one typical group: "They did not believe in any formal membership since that was the way of the world. They believed God kept a record of membership."[2]

Nevertheless, local fellowships existed, membership lists or not. There was, at least in the minds of those who were faithful in attendance and participation, a list of those who were the "ins" and the "outs." If it were not for the fact that there were these formally organized, informally organized, unorganized, or even disorganized congregations, there could have been no meetings to discuss how these groups might work together. We are thankful to the Head of the Church that through the Holy Spirit there was, during the period preceding 1884 and 1912, a growing sense of mission and a widening vision. This plus the failure to merge the Ansgar and Mission Synods and the subsequent dissolution of the Ansgar were two factors which prepared the way for the Boone meeting.

While there may not be any evidence of a direct influence, the early pioneers were greatly impressed by the teachings of John Nelson Darby (1800-1882) primarily in the area of prophecy. This is discussed in greater detail in another volume by the same author.[3]

Darby's opposition to denominationalism, formal church membership, non-scriptural titles, and a one-man ministry found a rapport among Scandinavian immigrants, not because this was new but because they had already started leaning toward a similar position before leaving the old country. His experience in first serving and then severing from the religious establishment was similar to their own at the hands of the State Church and their new discoveries in the reading of the Scripture. Darby was one of those instrumental in reviving an interest in Biblical prophecy especially as it pertained to the personal and premillennial return of Christ.

The Scandinavian community participated with great enthusiasm in the revival of studies in eschatology, the doctrine of the last things, sweeping across the American churches in the midst of great controversy rather than those emanating directly from Darby. It was a time of much publicized prophetic conferences. It was not that premillennialism was a new doctrine but that interest in the doctrine had been renewed. If anything was new, it was an extreme form of dispensationalism.

The first prophetic conference emphasizing premillennialism among the American believers was held in New York in 1879. This was while Princell was still a Lutheran pastor in New York. It is also significant that the president of the Lutheran Seminary during Princell's student days was not only a leader in the conference but authored the three-volume work on the Book of Revelation. He was Joseph A. Seiss and the work was called *Lectures on the Apocalypse*, published in 1869.

Pedersen published a similar book in Norwegian, *Syner fra Patmos*, in 1919 which, according to his own words in conversation, was inspired to a great extent by the works of Seiss. Princell must also have been inspired and turned his interest in a new direction for it has been reported that on his way to take over the presidency of Ansgar College, he stopped at Jamestown, New York, and preached two sermons, one on the structure of the church and the other on the soon return of Jesus Christ (1880)! These were, from that time on, his favorite subjects.

The prophetic conferences discussed and debated every phase of future events. A six-day conference, patterned after the American conference, held in Chicago (1881) dealt with such topics as the importance of the doctrine, the Kingdom of heaven, Israel, the Day of the Lord, Antichrist, signs of the times, etc. Franson, believing that the second coming was near, held short Bible courses in evangelism for men and women so that they might go out as evangelists. There was no time to delay. The King's errands required haste. This was before his trip to Europe and the shift of priorities from home evangelism to foreign missions. But whether at home or abroad, the time was short.

Premillennialism had a divisive effect on the Swedish community, as we shall note in another volume, which in turn somewhat affected the direction taken by the two Synods.

In Norway Franson outlined a plan for reaching every citizen with the Gospel within a year, a plan which was recently uncovered when an old, ignored chest in the basement of the Ansgar Publishing House was moved and opened during some building alterations. If Christ was coming soon, it became urgent that as many as possible be reached in as short a time as possible; but the task was too great for one local group. There needed to be cooperation and coordination. By 1883, these concerns became the topics for discussion. There was little disagreement over the need for working together but rather on how it might be accomplished.

In 1883 at a meeting in Boone the topic was similar, "How God's children might be able to unite or associate themselves in an evangelical work?" The answer, as adopted, was that "God's children in various places should unite to carry on a free Biblical work for the purpose of winning souls for God's glory." In October of 1883 another meeting was held in Chicago to consider the same subject. This has become known as the Bush Hall meeting. Participating, in addition to Princell and Martinson, were Skogsberg and Carl A. Bjork who became the leaders in the formation of the Covenant. In spite of differences about procedure, all shared a common concern. Also participating were the independents. At the Bush Hall meeting the participants were getting down to specifics—What is the Church?—When and by whom was it formed?—How is the local congregation organized?—The nature of the Church, her attributes, names, and basis for unity.—The relation of church members to each other. The details were reported in the paper for the whole Swedish community to consider. At this meeting a first step was taken in the appointment of a committee to plan another meeting which became the Boone meeting of 1884. Another conference was held in Moline in the summer of that year where the same subject was discussed. The purpose of a fellowship of congregations was clearly stated: "a united missionary work by individual Christian churches." It was there that Princell gave an added impetus to the idea, "The churches not only can and should work together in carrying out a missionary program both at home and abroad. That such cooperation and understanding are needed, both for preachers and in supporting such a work cannot be questioned . . . We should not follow the method of denominations in solving this problem, namely by multiplying organizations within organizations until a lot of machinery is needed."[4]

In these discussions two opposing philosophies began to crystallize, the one that the larger body should be composed of representatives of churches, their ministers and missionaries; and the other, that such an organization should be made up of member congregations. The differences may not seem great to us but in the 1880's it was serious business. Princell and Martinson were among the leading proponents of the first view. One should also mention Franson who, although he was abroad during the period these discussions and events took place, had written a series in *Chicago-Bladet* in which he contended that each local church should be its own denomination. On the other hand, men like Skogsberg and Bjork supported the concept of an association or union of the churches themselves.

Since the name of Bjork (1837-1916) will appear in the next chapter, it might be well to identify him more fully, for though he played an important role in the Mission and Ansgar Synod discussions and is well known in the Evangelical Covenant Church, he is an unknown in the Free Church. He served as chairman of the constitutional convention of the Covenant Church in 1885 and was its first president, a position which he held until 1910. Bjork emigrated from Sweden in 1864 and settled at Swede Bend, Iowa, where he plied his trade as a shoemaker and was also a gifted and successful preacher. Many in that part of western Iowa were converted under his ministry.

David Nyvall writes of Skogsberg and Bjork:

Bjork . . . was an aristocrat of a sort and a big man, partisan in his methods, with great personal congeniality. He was first and last a preacher, and a very clever man. Even his preaching was on the line of reasoning rather than emotional. He was quick in repartee as many stories testify. Among his equals Bjork lifted his head above the best. He had a much more immediate influence over those who stood next to him than he had over the crowd. In this as in many other things he was the opposite to Skogsberg . . . . who was strong with the crowd and somewhat lacking in the persuasive powers over those next in command. Bjork towered at the conferences where his will could be organized into official decision. Skogsberg had the ear of the people between conferences. He was largely an independent and somewhat vaguely supported by public opinion. Together they represented a centrepetal and a centrifugal power within the Covenant which was jointly beneficial. Bjork did not believe in competition. The churches and district unions (conferences) to him were agents at large with the simple duty to further the enterprise of the Covenant . . .[5]

Skogsberg writes of the time when the two men served in North and South Chicago. Since Skogsberg was given a choice, he selected the South side (1878) which he considered the younger of the two congregations. This was known as the Swedish Tabernacle. He also writes of forgetting much of what was discussed at the 1879 Conference of the Mission Synod because at an evening service in the presence of a full house he was united in marriage to one who became his life's partner. Bjork, "tied a knot, so strong that it could only be untied in death."[6]

In these two men, Princell and his colleagues had worthy adversaries.

A second development which put added pressure on the pioneers to consider bringing the groups together was the failure to merge the Mission and Ansgar Synods in 1878 and the anticipated dissolution of the Ansgar Synod a few months before the Boone conference. Committees representing both groups were appointed. They met, discussed, and prepared a recommendation for union. The efforts failed to materialize and the discussion of merger was formally dropped in 1879 though the matter was continually debated until the events of 1884 and 1885.

In the meantime, the Ansgar Synod was drifting farther away from Lutheran theology. Upon its dissolution, many of those who had been associated with the Synod were ready to join in the action taken at Boone.

Turning to the Norwegian-Danish Association, there was no suggestion that a national organization be formed for the purpose of sending missionaries abroad since the congregations were associated with the Scandinavian Alliance Mission (The Evangelical Alliance Mission) from its beginning. There was, however, the need for working together in home missions and evangelism.

Though the need was sensed, the reluctance to unite was slow in being overcome. The Eastern and Western Districts were organized in 1891 seven years after the first local congregations had been established. The two districts, which were first organized "for fellowship," began immediately to discuss how they could interest their people in home missions, enlarge the dimensions of the Free Church movement, and best provide Christian education for the children. This was accomplished, following the Congregational pattern, by State or District Missionary Societies. In their fear of denominationalism, they even hesitated to permit the two districts to be jointly responsible lest a form of central control develop. It was considered safer to keep the evangelistic efforts decentralized. The Western invited the Eastern to meet in 1898 to consider a merger. The invitation was rejected. The issue was revived in 1909 and the Association finally incorporated in 1912.

Even after the Boone meeting the Swedes were equally slow in formally organizing. A committee was appointed to plan the next meeting, a resolution on the structure of the church adopted, and plans initiated to send two missionaries to India. The plan to send the missionaries was aborted with the result that the first missionary enterprise was in China, not India. It was also agreed that "local churches should cooperate among themselves by means of conferences and societies as well as with individuals in whom they have confidence." It wasn't until twenty years had passed (1904) that serious consideration was given to incorporate resulting in the appointment of a committee, which apparently did nothing but was re-elected in 1905 and given a second chance. It responded by reporting favorably to the conference in 1906. The matter was referred to the affiliated congregations which held off the actual act of incorporation until 1908. There has been criticism among some of the descendants of the founders of the Mission Covenant that the Free Church chose 1884 and not 1908 as the year of beginning. Had they voted in 1884 to incorporate the entire action would have been inconsistent at that time with everything which had been debated up to and at that meeting. Further, it has been said that the Free Church is a "split-off" from the Covenant. I find it impossible to figure out how any organization founded in 1884 could be a "split-off" from one not founded until 1885.

This is not a new charge, merely a repetition of the many unfortunate charges and counter charges made in the beginning as one of the historians of the early days noted:

> From certain circles has come both in speech and in writing, the propaganda that the Evangelical Free Church is a splinter from a certain denomination. It is suggested that it is the final result of a divisive work being carried out by believers in this denomination. They therefore look upon the Free Church as the result of a schism and as such has no right to exist as an indigenous denomination.

He then goes on to list six reasons why this was not so. (1) The Ansgar Synod had been dissolved leaving a number of congregations, unwilling to become part of the Mission Synod, without any affiliation. This was likewise true of the leaders within the churches and synods. (2) Princell had, in *Chicago-Bladet*, proposed the type of Free Church adopted at Boone in 1884. (3) Frederick Franson had written a series proposing much the same long before 1884. (4) The great increase of immigrants, many of whom were converted in the Franson revivals in Sweden 1882-83. (5) The controversies in Sweden over the teachings on the atonement and baptism contributed to the decisions of 1884. (6) The matter was discussed long before the synod was dissolved.[7]

The incorporation statement of purpose is in line with the aims of both groups (Swedish and Norwegian-Danish) from the beginning: "To provide an alliance and a cooperation of independent Swedish congregations for the advancement of Christian faith and life in conformity with the teachings of the Holy Bible, through pursuance of Christian education and Christian missions at home and abroad; that is, in this and foreign countries."

There is one matter which is a disappointment to this writer. Why, if these were laymen's movements, were not more laymen involved in the organizational conference? One answer may be that in those days most of the leaders, especially in the Swedish Free Church, were unordained men. The idea of ordaining a man was slowly accepted and then left to local congregations lest a hierarchy develop.

Today, there are safeguards against the conferences being dominated by the clergy. At least one third of the membership of each board must be laymen and one third pastors. Pastors have voting rights as members of the Ministerial Association though limiting that to those who are actually pastors of Free Church congregations has been discussed. If it appears in the future that members of the Ministerial are about to have the majority in the voting membership of the conference, there is no doubt that the matter of limitation of voting rights will be reconsidered.

The Evangelical Free Church was and is to this day, not an organization of member congregations but a conference of voting delegates and ministers who constitute the denomination from one conference to the next. Should a serious emergency develop calling for denominational action it would be necessary to reassemble those who held voting rights at the previous conference. To ascertain who constitutes the Evangelical Free Church for any given year one does not look for the list of churches but the list of those who were given voting rights at the last previous conference. What then determined, and does so to this day, a congregation's right to representation at a national conference? The question is answered in the Bylaws:

> Membership in The Evangelical Free Church of America is available to such evangelical Christian churches of like faith and practice as shall recognize this organization, and adopt its principles and enter its fellowship by virtue of their acceptance by a district organization."[8]

This plan goes back to the beginning when the state and regional missionary organizations came into existence to carry out the program of evangelism (church extension). Technically, the congregations do not join the denomination but are recognized by the district conferences which in turn give the churches the right to participate in the National Conference.

The primary purpose of the national organization was to help the congregations better carry out the Great Commission and provide fellowship. It was started and is maintained as an organization for missions. In this, the parts are greater than the whole for without the parts the whole would never have come into existence nor would it have survived. The highest authority was and is vested in the local congregations whose delegates make the decisions of mutual concern in accordance with the purpose so clearly stated in the beginning and recognized for the last century:

> The Evangelical Free Church of America shall be an Association and Fellowship of independent congregations of like faith whose only objectives shall be the salvation of souls and the edification of believers in faith, hope and love.[9]

The pioneers used many methods in accomplishing this purpose. They soon took over the publishing of the periodicals, established schools to train workers, assisted in the founding of new congregations as stated specifically in today's articles of incorporation:

B. The Evangelical Free Church of America shall be involved in the following activities pursuant to these objectives:

1. To organize churches and Sunday schools and to establish and maintain Christian missionary work in the United States and other countries.

2. To promote mutual fellowship and harmony among the churches and to unite them for mutual activities beyond the scope and ability of a local congregation but having no controlling power over the internal affairs of such congregations.

3. To organize, build, administer and support schools and theological seminaries.

4. To educate and ordain ministers and missionaries when necessary, to assign missionaries to duty, and to recall them when necessary.

5. To build and maintain charitable and benevolent institutions.

6. To publish and distribute Christian literature.

7. (This paragraph is a legal statement as to buying and selling property and not pertinent to the present

discussion.)

    8. Any other such activities as deemed necessary that are related to the accomplishment of the objectives stated in A.[10]

The above outlined purposes and plans for their implementation reflect the views of both the Swedish and Norwegian-Danish groups. Once the language barriers disappeared it was only natural, with so much in common, for the two to merge in 1950. For details see the *Diamond Jubilee Story*. The wording of the purpose and its method of accomplishment were adopted at the merger conference. These were based on the original purposes as published at the beginning of both.

This then is the identity so long sought, so slowly recognized and adopted only after much prayer, discussion, and travail. God had to overrule. He provided the founders with wisdom beyond their considerable knowledge. Halleen put it well:

> The launching of the Free Church may be considered a result of daring rather than deliberate planning. Humanly speaking the founders seemed to have stumbled into the work. They stumbled into a movement which in a few years they absorbed and used to telling success. By the grace of God they were, however, divinely ordained to lead the new movement into larger fields and greater activities.[11]

They had based their conclusions on what they read in the Scriptures and what they had seen in other groups with similar or different church polity.

This is our inheritance. We have kept the capital of that inheritance intact, invested it wisely and used the returns to lead, as above quoted, "into larger fields and greater activities." At least this is true up to the centennial in 1984.

We still follow the slogan introduced by Franson: the congregation can be its own synod and should join with others to carry out the Lord's work.

The local church still retains the right to call its own

pastor, man or woman.

The local church still retains the right to ordain its own pastor, man or woman.

The local church retains the right to send out its own missionaries to the fields at home and abroad but does so through the fellowship of churches thus following the very principle laid down in 1884 as being the purpose of a denomination. However, missionaries are not commissioned at a general conference but in their home churches.

There is no unified budget calling for unspecified giving to the national organization. The support of workers as well as institutions is according to the wishes of the individuals and members.

The congregations are not taxed. Goals may be set but the response must be clearly voluntary.

Not even the decisions of the general conference are legally binding upon the affiliated congregations. They support voluntarily. However, one of the tragedies is that some local pastors and/or congregations, to prove this right to dissent, ignore all decisions and appeals for projects which are listed in the very purposes of the denomination.

Separate administrative boards are chosen for the purposes listed in the Bylaws. Their members are elected by the delegates for three-year terms and limited to two terms to prevent a hierarchy from developing.

The department heads must face the conference every three years to give the delegates an opportunity to approve or disapprove their leadership.

The Board of Directors is a coordinating, rather than a governing body, and has no authority over local congregations.

The delegates to the conference have the right to nominate candidates for all of the offices equal to the number proposed by the committees or boards.

The Editor is not hired by a board but elected for a three-year term and so is answerable to all the churches. We noted in the previous chapter that the papers published before the denominations were born in Scandinavia and the United States were owned and edited by individuals and were not responsible to the churches. This proved unsatisfactory, once the associations were formed. It wasn't long before the denominations in Scandinavia began publishing their own papers. In America, the Norwegian-Danish Association took over the editing and publishing of the *Evangelisten* and the Swedish Free Church eventually did the same with the *Chicago-Bladet*. To be the official organ, it would have to serve the entire constituency.

This writer, who together with his colleagues on the committee carried the responsiblity for the preparation of the merger plan adopted in 1950, studied carefully the early history and traditions of both groups and were dedicated to bringing about the union only if nothing of the precious inheritance of both the Swedish and Norwegian-Danish Free Churches was lost through the merger proceedings. The threat remains, and a haunting one it is to those dedicated to these principles of church polity, that the inheritance could be squandered whether it be the doctrinal base, the church structure, or both. Other choices of denominational and local church structures, even within evangelical circles, are available to those dissatisfied with the congregational system without anyone having to rewrite the history of the Free Churches or change the polity. While the doctrinal statement declares that the local congregation has the right to handle its own affairs there are two, sometimes overlooked, restrictions on that freedom—"its own affairs"—"under Christ."

Congregations and pastors have freedom of choice whether or not they would be part of or serve the Free Church. But they should not decide to reform, rebuild, or rewrite the principles and polity even in the "independent" local church. That would be to enter the fold another way rather than through the door. That door is clearly marked, "The Evangelical Free Church of America shall be an Association and Fellowship of independent congregations of *like faith.*" And again, "such other churches of *like faith* and *practice* as shall *recognize this organization* and *adopt its principles* may also enter this fellowship."

These principles must be taught our children in our homes and churches and to our students at the seminary. Each generation must know the capital assets of the inheritance and how it can be invested so as to increase its influence.

The Ministerial Association, organized ten years later, followed the pattern of the American Congregational Church, and though autonomous also includes self-imposed restrictions: "The purpose of this organization shall be to promote and extend the work of the Lord by the proclamation of the Gospel; also to encourage Christian fellowship among those ministernig in the Evangelical Free Church of America and in a wholesome and loving manner build one another up in the faith . . . members are expected to live Godly lives and proclaim faithfully the Word of God within the *historic framework of the Evangelical Free Church of America"* . . . . *An applicant for membership "must work in harmony with the principles of the Evangelical Free Church of America."*[12]

Princell often used the illustration of five brothers, one of whom did not get along with the other four. The four united in purpose and effort started to build a house. At night, the fifth brother would come and tear down in a brief time what it had taken four all day to build. Many beloved pioneers worked hard to put it all together. One can tear apart in a short time what it has taken a century to build. We therefore need watchmen as well as workmen, and congregations who are grateful for the heritage and determined not to squander it.

FOOTNOTES—CHAPTER VII

1. The *Golden Jubilee of the Swedish Evangelical Free Church*, 1934, p. 16.
2. Carlsen, Nils C., *Liv og Virksomhet i Herren's Vingaard*, Evangelisten's Forlag, Chicago, 1928, p. 9.
3. In the book, *This We Believe*, the author has discussed more fully the views on eschatology.
4. Much of the material on the 1884 conference is provided by the *Diamond Jubilee Story*, back issues of *Chicago-Bladet* and minutes of the succeeding conferences.
5. Nyvall, David, *The Evangelical Covenant*, Covenant Press, Chicago, 1954, p. 77, 78.
6. Skogsberg, E. August, *Minnen och Upplevelser*, Vekobladets Trykeri, Minneapolis (1915?), p. 179.
7. *Minneskrift*. Thirtieth Anniversary book by the Swedish Evangelical Free Church, 1914, p. 7, 8.
8. The Evangelical Free Church Bylaws Section I on membership.
9. *Ibid.*, Articles of Incorporation, Section II A on objectives.
10. *Ibid.*, Section II B.
11. Golden Jubilee, op. cit., p. 13.
12. From the revised Bylaws of the Ministerial Association.

Chapter VIII

GOOD FENCES MAKE GOOD NEIGHBORS

The failure of the Ansgar and Mission Synods to get together and the subsequent formation of the two Swedish denominations gives additional support to the concept of church polity established at the meeting in Boone in 1884.

Likewise, the formation of the Norwegian-Danish district societies apart from the American Congregational Church but with the support of the teachers at the seminary and the man assigned as superintendent of the work among them, helped prepare the way for an independent denomination entirely apart from the "generous uncle." It is interesting to note that though the annual reports of the Congregational Home Mission Society listed the names of the Norwegian-Danish Congregational Churches, the Society never recognized the Eastern and Western Districts nor the national association once it was organized.

The problem among the Swedes was quite different. Though the issues had changed by the time of the conventions in 1884 and 1885, the seeds of discontent and continued division were sown when the two Synods were first formed in 1873 and 1874. The Mission Synod was organized first. The Ansgar was formed more or less in protest over the former's refusal to affiliate with the American

Northern Illinois Lutheran Synod. Both, as we have noted, eventually wished to disavow the Augsburg Confession, following the influence of the Waldenstrom theory of the atonement. Both had made the mistake of including the confession in their articles of incorporation making it necessary to dissolve the corporation before a change could be made. The Mission Synod tried to amend by adding John 3:16 only to find that illegal.

But even before Princell moved into the Ansgar picture with his fear of denominationalism there were signs of a change in the thinking of the Ansgar leadership. They decided in 1882 to withdraw from the affiliation with the Northern Ilinois Synod but still could not alter or drop the Lutheran confession. Earlier than that (1880) consideration had been given to a congregational form of church government by the adoption of a new policy on church polity:

> "This synod shall not be or function as a denominational structure to admit congregations and ordain pastors, but as an association of Christian brothers who shall work together for the proclamation of the Gospel according to the directives of God's Word and the pertinent circumstances at hand . . . this synod or association will leave local congregations completely free in all respects whether in the calling of preachers or pastors (elders) and other ministers (deacons), or in the installation (ordination) of these into the ministry through prayer and the laying on of hands.[1]

One would think such a radical change might be well publicized. The proposal was apparently premature as it had the support of only a small minority. Through the power of the press, Martenson slowed the idea down by insisting that the Ansgar Synod must first be dissolved. The proposal had its own content for self-destruction in that it made no provision for inter-church relations or any basis for a relationship with the still existing Synod members. Isolation was confused with independence.

The difference between the two Synods became more easily identified in the failure to merge the two in 1879. A joint committee brought recommendations that "a union can be brought about most conveniently by dissolving both synods and by drawing up and adopting a new constitution for a united organization . . . based on the Word of God!" The matter was tabled by both groups. Bjork, then president of the Mission Synod, responded to the approach of a merger by saying, "Our brothers of the Ansgar Synod have, with their proposal for union, clearly led us to understand that they consider us Christians and that they have unquestioned confidence in us. Because of this, they, in their Synod, feel pushed aside, like a limb separated from the body."

He also said, "Perhaps they now see the error in this respect and the manner in which they have carried on their work, organized congregations, established a school, and sent out ministers. In my opinion as well as in the opinion of many of our brethren which I know, all this has seemed a deviation from the Scripture and pure Christian brotherly love. Therefore, I see no possibility of a union until I see satisfactory evidence of an honorable desire to repent and that this desire is in actuality honest."[2]

Karl Olsson suggests that "Bjork's strategy is clear. Ansgar has come to the Mission Synod as an equal. Bjork casts it in the role of a prodigal son who should ask forgiveness. In this sort of relationship there can be no talk of union, only incorporation."[3]

Bjork believed, and this is the position which has stopped every attempt at merging the Free Church and Covenant, that only the Ansgar Synod should be dissolved and the affiliated congregations then join the Mission Synod under its constitution. "Our friends," he said, "are so worn and wearied by novelties that when they have now achieved something which is Scriptural they do not want to relinquish it in order to throw themselves into an unseen confusion, for our Synod is founded on the Word of God and is legally constituted."[4]

The tensions continued. We have reported on the Bush

Hall meeting which resulted in appointing a committee to plan for another conference the next year to continue the study of church polity. This resulted in the Boone meeting of October 14-19, 1884, to which all interested parties had been invited. Those in attendance did not know that at that very time (Oct. 18) a self-appointed committee was meeting in Chicago to plan another meeting somewhat in competition but with a similar purpose. A letter was sent to leaders and congregations in both, dated November 1st, calling upon the Ansgar and Mission Synods to consider a joint meeting at which a plan of union might be achieved among those pastors and churches desiring such. This came as a disturbing shock to those who had met in Boone. As a result of that letter, a meeting was called for Chicago, February 18-25, 1885, at which the Mission Covenant was organized. The churches in the Mission Synod did not dissolve the Synod but merely transferred their affiliation to the new corporation, leaving the old still existing on paper. Thus they were also free to drop or amend the Augsburg Confession.

The fires of schism became more intense. The Boone committee, instead of waiting until another year had passed, as planned, called a special meeting in March (25-30) held at the American Congregational Church in Minneapolis. The topics discussed had an additional meaning in light of the events in Chicago in February: How can a Christian non-denominational and non-sectarian work best be organized?—Is it necessary that congregations unite in order to conduct a united missionary endeavor?—How can churches and preachers overcome the distances between them and become better acquainted; interact beneficially; and share, with faith in each other, the work of saving sinners and edifying the children of God?

Whether the continued division of the two schools of thought—a denomination composed of delegates, pastors, etc., or of member churches—was providential or a tragedy, we'll have to leave to others to decide. I find it difficult as one who has spent fifty years in the work of the Free Church and who has many friends in the Covenant to be objective. I also have a sentimental problem which makes an objective conclusion difficult. My mother and father, in widely separated communities, were converted in the revivals sweeping Norway at the turn of the century. As lonely immigrants, they found each other in a Covenant Church in northern Minnesota and after moving to the city of Minneapolis attended a Swedish Free Church until they became charter members of a Norwegian-Danish Free Church when that was organized. My spiritual heritage comes from the three denominations.

The relationship between the two is today far more cordially fraternal than in the early days. They work together in Zaire. Both belong to the International Federation of Free Evangelical Churches. Leaders, pastors, members of both are good friends. However, the primary difference continued to plague attempts at merger. Feelings were not expressed as charitably as they would be today had such discussions continued.

As examples of how the charges and counter charges went we mention but two. Bowman, president of the Covenant 1927-33 writes:

> The "Free element, which finally united the Swedish Free Church of the United States, took from the start a less friendly attitude toward the Mission Covenant. For some time the prevailing opinion among "the Free" was that they represented a more spiritual Christianity and that those who sympathized with the Mission Covenant were more worldly-minded. Not all of "the Free" however, allowed themselves to take such a view of the situation. Fortunately such comparisons are very seldom heard at the present time. Yet, while such ideas prevailed they had a tendency to create a deeper sense of division, to encourage unfriendly feeling, and to separate the two groups more fully.[5]

There is no doubt but what some of the Free Church people thought they were more spiritual and said so.

Bowman, apparently basing his conclusion on Princell's

view favoring the final annihilation of the ungodly, accused the Free Churches of believing the same. Incidentally, in spite of Princell's great leadership in church polity, the Free Church of today does not follow his teachings on the above, or on soul sleep or the atonement.[6]

Bowman's charge appears in the Swedish edition of his history (1907) but was omitted from the English edition in 1925.

The Ministerial Association, at its meeting in 1908, responded to the charge with the following resolution:

We, the members of the Swedish Evangelical Free Mission Ministerial Association, assembled for our annual meeting in Minneapolis, Minn. June 29-30, 1908, wish to present a strong protest against the accusation of heresy appearing in Pastor C. V. Bowman's book, "The Mission Friends in America," concerning the Free Mission. On page 264 of this book the author states: "Within the Covenant the belief in everlasting punishment is quite general. Within the Free Mission, on the other hand, belief in the annihilation of the wicked is generally widespread." With the knowledge we have of our field and the people with whom we work, we consider ourselves more competent and qualified to judge what is generally believed and what is not believed among our ministers and in our congregations than someone outside of our work could possibly be. According to our opinion it could just as well be said that the universalism of Ekman is widespread in the Mission Covenant in Sweden and here in our country inasmuch as it has become known and strongly discussed through various books and papers, as to state that belief in the annihilation of the wicked is widespread in the Free Mission because there have been lively discussions of these teachings among us.

In general the doctrine of annihilation is considered a heresy among us. A general conference of the Free Mission has expressed itself against the doctrine and rejected any responsibility for such teachings. Such teachings are refuted and our people are warned concerning them with as much earnestness as is done among other groups.

In view of this, we consider the author to have grossly misrepresented and hurt us. We trust that, since we recognize the author to be an honest and God-fearing brother, he will consider it his duty to make the necessary correction.[7]

The slogan "tell it like it is" is not new! In spite of wild talk against each other at times, underneath was a desire to get together but that desire was not strong enough to overcome the major obstacle, that of denominational structure. Princell, as early as 1886, proposed a merger but on his own terms and Franson went a step farther by working on a plan to enlarge the union to include the Swedish Congregationalists, of which there were more churches than in the other two combined.

Sincere attempts were made but failed on the question of the relationship of a local congregation to the larger body. It brings us back to the debates in England and New England nearly three hundred years earlier. Are the parts greater than the whole or is the whole greater than the parts? In *This We Believe* I presented the resolutions, reports and decisions which bear repeating in this context.

The first plan (1886) was to seek union only in the areas of a common school for the training of pastors, a hymnal and an address book.

J. G. Princell and A. A. Anderson were chosen to represent the Swedish Free Church on a committee consisting of representatives from each group. This committee felt that no common school for the training of preachers could be established without some understanding first as to the details and the basis for such a united effort.

In 1909 a new committee on union presented a comprehensive resolution including a declaration of principles for unity, a presentation of areas of cooperation (home missions, foreign missions, schools, benevolent institutions, etc.), a plan for merger, and a tentative constitution. This was adopted by the Free Church. The committee reported in 1910, 1911, and 1912 that in the absence of an approval by one of the other groups nothing further had been done. In 1913 a communication was received from the Swedish Mission Covenant. That, together with the resolutions which followed, revealed the real difference—the concern for the guaranteed independence of the local church.

The committee reviewed at length the many things the group had in common. The Covenant supported this but suggested, in view of certain legal complications, that the constitution and name of that organization become the guide for the united group. This the Free Church was willing to do with the reservation as follows, which again calls attention to a basic difference:

> Concerning membership and representation, we believe that we should require that all congregations which work in harmony with and contribute to the united organization should be given equal representation, regardless of whether they can or wish to formally join the organization as such.
>
> Inasmuch as most of the Free Churches have a paragraph in their constitution which prohibits affiliation with a denomination, it is impossible for them to formally affiliate with the organization if two or three members are opposed to it without losing their property. Therefore we believe that the congregations which do not formally join the organization should be given the same privileges as those which do affiliate as long as they demonstrate their interest and sense of belonging to the organization. (Para. III of the Committee Report—1913)

After several years of discussion the matter was dropped in 1914. At that conference a most enthusiastic communication was read from the Covenant members of the Unity Committee urging approval of merger plans and making a plea that the difference of opinion as to a new name be held in abeyance until more important issues were ironed out. However, the Free Church replied with the recommendation that the matter be dropped.

The idea of a merger was revived in 1919 with an exchange of telegrams by the two conferences. The first was from the Covenant conference at Rockford, Ill., to the Free Church conference at Holdrege as follows:

> The Covenant sends a brotherly greeting to the Free Church and expresses unanimously a wish that a practical union between the two bodies may be realized.

The Free Church replied:

Your telegram was received with pleasure and its contents acted upon. A union committee was appointed. Wishing God's blessing upon your Conference.

The merger committee presented a long resolution to the next conference outlining a proposal for union. It included the suggestion that a referendum be held by the churches to be completed in time for the 1921 conventions and that at these a ⅔ vote in favor be required to warrant the calling of a merger conference. The conference voted 49 to 48 in favor of the resolution! The Covenant voted 248-7 in favor of referring the matter to the churches. The opposition argued that the proposals were not specific enough in the following areas—the merging of schools, the relation of local congregations to the new organization and the voting rights of those churches forbidden by their own constitutions to formally join a denomination. The committee was asked to prepare a constitution for the next annual meeting. In 1921 the committee recommended that without considering a constitution the matter be referred to the churches for a vote. This was done. The report in 1922 indicates that only 61 of the 106 churches responded. Not exactly an enthusiastic response! Three refused to vote, 38 voted in favor and 21 against. The vote of individuals ɩ s 1235 to 591! So the matter stands to this day. (Covenant, 172-80 in favor.)

One is often asked, "Will there be a merger of the Free Church and Covenant?" One man's opinion, that of the president of the Covenant, Clarence Nelson in 1961, is significant:

The Covenant made a bona fide overture to the Evangelical Free Church in the 1920's for merging these two denominations. The Free Church did not accept the proposal, and although there are still some voices that continue to urge such a merger, action appears less likely now than ever. This is due, I believe, in no small measure to the differences that characterize the two denominations in the area of the theology of the church and the sacraments.[8]

Nelson mentions two roadblocks to merger—the one has stood in the way since the beginning. A model constitution for local Free Church congregations states:

"The church shall remain free and independent and shall not join itself to any other denomination or synod. It shall remain its own highest authority and shall conduct its business through its business sessions. The church shall cooperate with the Evangelical Free Church of America and its branches, and with the Evangelical Free Church _____ District Conference by sending delegates to conferences, supporting Home and Foreign Missions and uniting in many mutual efforts for the furtherance of the gospel as the church itself may officially decide." (Article VII on Standing.)

The one suggested by the Covenant reads:

"This church is affiliated with the Evangelical Covenant Church of America and its _____ Conference and is pledged to support the program, policies and institutions inherent in the fellowship."

Karl Olsson, while president of North Park, in commenting on the difference wrote:

Why, after so much talk and so much genuine feeling, did the love merger with the Free Church fail to materialize?

The causes are complex, but a careful reading of the history during the years 1885-1922 makes it clear that the time had brought a fixation of identities.

To begin with differences had been largely in the area of polity. The Boone split-off had come because the Free Church wanted a democratic rather than a republican polity. It did not want its deliberative body to be composed solely of representatives from member churches—a position espoused by the founders of the Covenant. It followed that the Free Church did not want the deliberate body to ordain and license pastors or to perform other denominational functions. It wanted its character to remain that of a mission association.

The Covenant on the other hand was loath to dissolve its corporate structure and particularly balked at a proposal that together with the Free Church it adopt the name "The Swedish United Mission Church of America."[9]

In this he is correct, but his second observation is open to question. He continues:

But more than polity became involved. There was a fixation also of theological identity. In the 35-year period between 1885 and 1920 the majority of Covenant pastors, although retaining their zeal for awakening and regeneration, became more discriminating in their doctrinal orientation. They stood closer than the Free Church to developments in the Covenant of Sweden and were not unaffected by a growing sophistication in the ranks of the latter. The Free Church on the other hand lived closer to the influences emanating from Moody Bible Institute in Chicago and was more amenable to the positions eventually espoused by the World's Christian Fundamentals Association. It is hence possible to detect in the efforts at rapprochement in the period 1915-20 a growing theological divergence which was to play a significant part in the developments which reached a climax in Omaha in 1928.

Gustaf F. Johnson of the Free Church became a Covenant pastor in 1914 and lent his personal prestige to the merger efforts. But although a considerable segment of the Covenant clergy was polarized around Johnson in this period, the Free Church could not have believed that he represented the majority of Covenanters. Their reluctance to approve the merger referendum of 1921-22 was unquestionably rooted in their fear of being swallowed up by the numerically stronger Covenant. But mingled with that fear was a growing resistance to the Covenant image.

In any event, the question of a merger with the Evangelical Free Church has been a dead issue for over four decades.[10]

He overlooked the fact that while no leader of the EFCA was active in the leadership of the WCFA, Dr. Paul Rood, a Covenant pastor, served as head of the organization for many years.

Nelson mentions another roadblock, namely the sacraments. This difference is not of recent origin, although it has become more apparent in recent years. Bowman notes this back in 1925:

"Then, too, certain doctrinal differences developed which gave the two groups their own peculiar color. Thus the Free Church by common practice sanctions the baptism of adults and very few believe in infant baptism. In the Mission Covenant the great majority hold that infant baptism is right and only a smaller number believe that the baptism of adults is to be preferred. Yet neither one of the groups makes the acceptance of this or that view concerning baptism conditional for membership in the churches. Other less marked doctrinal differences also are noticeable. Still the existing differences are small compared with the many things held in common by the Free Church and the Mission Covenant."[11]

Since the purpose of this volume, as repeated often on these pages, is not to discuss the doctrines, except the one dealing with the church polity, we review only what Nelson called the "differences" that characterize the two denominations in the area of theology concerning the church.

In response to the proposal by the Free Church in 1909 the Covenant suggested that the constitution and the name of the Covenant be the pattern for the united group. This sounds like the Mission Synod's response to Ansgar on incorporation by the one joining the other rather than the merger of two equals. The new approach in 1914 did not eliminate the old problem. The Covenant voted in favor but the Free Churches could not accept a plan which took away the long sought after and struggled for identity.

Karl Olsson was asked to present a paper on the Similarities and Differences between the member churches of the International Federation in America while a European theologian was asked to prepare one on the Similarities and Differences between those in Europe. These were to be among a number of papers presented at the Theological Conference held at North Park College and Trinity Evangelical Divinity School in 1971 which brought together representatives of all the denominations in the Federation of Free Evangelical Churches. Olsson concluded by a look into the future:

> Because I am not a risking person and a very poor prophet, I can do no more than suggest directions in which the two denominations may go. In addition to maintaining its constituency, the Free Church may, because of its firm doctrinal stand, have an opportunity to minister to groups who are

looking for both disestablishment and Scriptural authority . . . Thousands of young people have been turned off by the bland and indecisive amiability of the secularized church and are looking for clearer marching orders.

The Covenant will probably have a different role. It cannot be so doctrinally unequivocal as the Free Church. It cannot draw with such simple, bold strokes. By character and tradition, it is committed not to doctrine but to life and relationships. Thus it commends itself to people who have come through a convertive crises and are looking for a fellowship in which there is evangelical life and warmth and a serious commitment to the Scriptures but also freedom to differ theologically and to grow relationally. It may also be able to minister to people disenchanted with liberal churches because of their lack of life and to those who are disenchanted with Fundamentalist churches because of the lack of freedom.

Both the Free Church and Covenant are conservative, evangelical denominations, but each will have a different function. They have enough commonality to meet together amicably but too many differences to invite the intimacy of union. Hence, it may continue to be true for these denominations that good fences make good neighbors.

Good fences make good neighbors! This same sentiment was expressed by a Free Church historian who wrote in 1924:

> The harmony and the cooperation of these organizations have been at their best when no mention has been made of a formal union. In this great land of ours, with its millions of inhabitants, there are ample fields for those who wish to preach Christ, and may good will and harmony be prevalent among the workers in the different fields until the coming of our Lord Jesus Christ.[12]

This brings us to a matter which must not be overlooked. While the identity of the church structure was established it was not to the downgrading of all others. It was stated often that while they agreed that the local congregation was to be composed only of believers, they recognized that all believers, everywhere, were members of the body of Christ.

The Norwegians and Danes had early endorsed the Congregational Doctrinal Statement which declared, "We believe that the Church of Christ, visible and spiritual, comprises all true believers . . . " The doctrinal statement of the Norwegian-Danish group, adopted when the national organization was formed, declares, "We believe that as many as by faith receive Jesus Christ as their Savior and Lord are born again and are given the witness of the Holy Spirit, and become children and heirs of God, and joint-heirs with Jesus Christ." The meeting at Boone passed a resolution which included, "The Church of God on earth consists of the entire multitude of converted, born-again to Christ baptized persons, wherever such may dwell." And, finally, in the statement as adopted by both denominations at the time of the merger the same is reiterated, "We believe that the true church is composed of all such persons who through saving faith in Jesus Christ have been regenerated by the Holy Spirit and are united together in the body of Christ, of which He is the head."

In all of the discussions insisting on the independence of the local church and strong attacks on the "sin of denominationalism" our founders never lost sight of the great truth that the body of Christ is greater than a local body of believers and the denominations with which they are affiliated. This is expressed with clarity from the beginning, yes, even before the beginning.

Franson was emphatic:

All God's children in all localities throughout the world have a natural oneness together in the bonds of love and peace, because they are all the children of the same Father, they all make up the Bride of Jesus, have the same Holy Spirit, the same Word to lead them, and they are all aiming for the same heaven. As such, they are responsive to each other, sense their participation with each other and, when the need arises, seek in all respects to help each other voluntarily, as they did in the days of the apostles (Acts 11:29). But, in addition, they are also—and that as a matter of course—joined together in their common task for the Lord . . . because of which they rejoice together in each other's victories . . . and intercede together concerning each other's burdens.

148

Near the end of the article he states, "All those who join themselves together in independent local churches must be careful to show, both by their deeds and by their fruits, that they are one with all of God's children."[13]

Franson at that time (1880-81) was far more independent than those meeting in Boone where they recognized a need for churches working together to carry out the mission of Christ.

He also wrote in the same series of articles, "Today what we see about us are congregations formally affiliated with one another . . . something about which the Bible says nothing!" Had he been at Boone instead of Europe in 1884 there might not have been the fine resolution on the church. However, anti-denominational though he was in his writings, he helped organize two Presbyterian churches in Utah in the interest of the few converts among the Swedes and Danes so they might have a flock of believers with whom to unite. Sometimes his practicality overruled his ecclesiology!

One might ask, if they had the conviction that all believers are members of Christ's body why did the Norwegians and Danes not join the American Congregational Church? We have alluded to the increasing theological changes of the latter; but there was also an emotional reason. They were afraid of anything American whether in the practices of the church or in the life-style of her members.

They were even against the Swedes! The failure of the merger attempt started in 1934 was more a matter of emotions than doctrine. The bitterness of the older immigrants from Norway and Denmark against Sweden was deep and not without foundation. The jokes about the Swedes and Norsemen were not amusing to them.

Let's take a brief look at history. For centuries Norway had been the pawn of the great European powers. She was united with Denmark in 1450. Following the Reformation, Norway sank almost to the level of a province; her fleet and army decayed, and her language gave place to Danish. Danes took over the higher posts of her administrators. Her churches and monasteries were sacked and Danes were installed as pastors under the Lutheran system following the Reformation. On May 17, 1814, Norway adopted its own constitution but did not acquire complete freedom. She was taken from Denmark and given to Sweden. The latter was a result of the Treaty of Kiel (1814) as a reward for fighting against Napoleon. Denmark had chosen the losing side. This transfer was done without any consultation with the Norwegians. Until 1905 the King of Sweden ruled Norway as well as Sweden even though Norway considered herself a duly constituted nation. As Norway's nationalism became stronger her opposition to Sweden grew.

My own father, a Norwegian, grew up on the border with Sweden and had stories of the border skirmishes. At the Folke Museum in Oslo there are a number of houses moved from several communities. One from my father's region has a tower on the roof with windows on all sides. At the foot of the ladder, hanging on the wall, one will see old guns. If the visitor should ask the hostess what they were for, she will reply, "To shoot bears and Swedes." Swedish soldiers would sneak across to steal fruit from the trees and vegetables out of the gardens. Even though they were not authorized to do so and would be punished by their commanding officers if caught, the tensions became more dangerous. Then came the great day of independence in 1905. It must be remembered that when the earliest leaders and people came to these shores their country was still under Sweden; but the leaders of the revival movement in all three countries maintained fraternal, unofficial relations with each other.

Some may ask, how come the Danes and the Norwegians could get together but neither with the Swedes? Norway's break with Denmark had taken place in 1814, and the hard days of the 16th to 18th centuries were mostly forgotten. In many communities, especially in New England, the Danes were fewer than the Norwegians and since they used a common language at that time it was convenient to worship together. We should also be reminded that the first head of the Norwegian-Danish department of the Chicago Theological Seminary was a Dane and so was the founder of the Swedish Ansgar Synod.

It is interesting to observe that the members appointed to the first merger committee from the Norwegian side had been born and spent their youth in Norway during the Swedish "occupation." Although this fact was not the main reason for the failure, some of these had a strong nationalistic bias. One of the primary reasons was the recommendation that the foreign missions program of the Swedish Free Church be placed under the Evangelical Alliance Mission. While I would not question the motives, it is, nevertheless, significant that some of the members of the joint committee were also members of the TEAM Board. Swedish Free Church missionaries on the various fields took part in the referendum and the vote in total revealed dissatisfaction with the plan. By 1939 the referendum was completed with results even less favorable than the vote on the Free Church-Covenant plan of 1922. From the Norwegian-Danish side only 22 out of 60 churches responded, 10 for, 9 against, 3 uncommitted; and from the Swedish side, 65 out of 120 responded with 55 voting in favor.

The decade that followed saw a number of changes. Both denominations gradually dropped the old country languages; the people and leaders in both groups became better acquainted as they moved out of their ethnic enclaves and on to peninsulas which began to reach into the American scene. The two schools, one in Minneapolis and one in Chicago, merged in 1946. A partnership was formed for publications. It is also significant that two of the three members from each denomination serving on the second merger committee were American born and free from the trauma of the old country experiences. There was, however, a new feeling of antagonism caused by events in Norway during the Nazi occupation in World War II and the neutrality of Sweden. But it was primarily, and understandably, in the hearts of those who knew by experience Norway's past history. But the resistance was not strong and the concern for the Lord's work overcame the little reluctance that remained. The vote at the conference of the Swedish Evangelical Free Church of America was 196 to 13 in favor and at the meeting of the Norwegian-Danish Association 73-5 in favor. This was the vote of the delegates, missionaries, and members of the Ministerial. Not all of the last two groups actually represented churches. Of the churches represented all had, in the referendum, voted in favor—a unanimous response!

Halleen with his gift of oratory, sense of humor, knowledge of history, and insight as well as foresight summarized the merger beautifully in his address at the first great united meeting following the vote by the two denominations to merge:

> I am looking west tonight. I feel that I am the connecting link between yesteryear and today . . . It is an honor to be a Norwegian—nearly as much as to be a Swede. By tomorrow we'll all be Americans.

It has been said that the Evangelical Free Church is a theological rather than an ecclesiastical body. Thus, as Karl Olsson reports in his paper, in the Covenant one can be "tried" for disloyalty to the "body mystique" but not for heresy (there is no detailed creed) whereas in the Free Church one can be tried for heresy but not for disloyalty.

For this reason the Evangelical Free Church has no inhibitions in relating to evangelicals be they members of a denomination which has a congregational, presbyterian or episcopal form of government. The bond is a common faith, not a common church polity. No, fences are not eliminated, but there is cooperation without compromise.

That is why the Evangelical Free Church was among the first to join the National Association of Evangelicals—why it has provided leadership in that area—why local pastors and people have no hesitation to join in the crusades of Billy Graham and other evangelical inter-church efforts—why they are so generous in supporting other evangelical causes.

It now has a sense of security as far as the structural identity is concerned. It does not fear that working with those in other church structures will destroy or weaken its own congregational system for which it so long sought and for which it fought. Any threat to the church polity will come from within—from some who may have entered not fully committed to that identity and so seek to change it locally. If such changes were permitted, the next step would be to change the structure nationally. Then much of the inheritance would be lost and this book will become meaningless.

The identity was now fixed. Both the Norwegian-Danish and Swedish Free Church in the merger proceedings of 1947-50 had the same fear—not doctrine, not personalities; but would a merger cause either group to give up any part of its identity? They became convinced, after much study and even the failure in 1939, that the identity would remain and even be enhanced! And so be it! Amen!

I love Thy kingdom, Lord, The house of Thine abode,
The Church our blest Redeemer saved With His own
precious blood.

I love Thy Church, O God! Her walls before Thee stand,
Dear as the apple of Thine eye and graven on Thy hand.

For her my tears shall fall; For her my prayers ascend;
To her my cares and toils be giv'n; Till toils and cares shall
end.

Beyond my highest joy I prize her heav'nly ways,
Her sweet communion, solemn vows, Her hymns of love
and praise.

Sure as Thy truth shall last, To Zion shall be giv'n
The brightest glories earth can yield, And brighter bliss of
heav'n.

—Timothy Dwight

FOOTNOTES—CHAPTER VIII

1. Erixon, Karl, *Smaa Reisebrev, Chicago-Bladet,* September 17, 1880. Erixon was president of the Ansgar Synod.
2. *Missions-Wannen,* January, 1979.
3. Olsson, Karl, *By One Spirit,* Covenant Press, Chicago, 1962. p. 264.
4. *Missions-Wannen,* op. cit.
5. Bowman, C. B., *The Mission Covenant of America,* Covenant Book Concern, Chicago, 1925, p. 216 (English translation)
6. *Ibid.,* p. 264 (Swedish, 1907) Minneapolis, Veckoblad Publishing Co.
7. From the minutes of the 1908 Ministerial Conference. The Ekman referred to was E. J. Ekman, the first president of the Covenant of Sweden.
8. *Covenant Companion,* July 20, 1961
9. *Ibid.,* April 3, 1964
10. *Ibid.*
11. Bowman, C. V., op. cit., p. 153
12. Modig, August H., *Ebenezer,* p. 7, Published on the occasion of the fortieth anniversary of the Swedish Evangelical Free Church of America.
13. *Chicago-Bladet,* December 1880, January 1881. A series on the Biblical Pattern of the Local Church.

INDEX

155

125527

LINCOLN CHRISTIAN UNIVERSITY

3 4711 00230 6316